FOCUS ON

CHAPLIN

FILM FOCUS

Ronald Gottesman and Harry M. Geduld
General Editors

THE FILM FOCUS SERIES PRESENTS THE BEST THAT HAS BEEN
WRITTEN ABOUT THE ART OF FILM AND THE MEN WHO CREATED
IT. COMBINING CRITICISM WITH HISTORY, BIOGRAPHY, AND ANAL-
YSIS OF TECHNIQUE, THE VOLUMES IN THE SERIES EXPLORE THE
MANY DIMENSIONS OF THE FILM MEDIUM AND ITS IMPACT ON
MODERN SOCIETY.

DONALD W. McCAFFREY *is Associate Professor English and
Teacher of Cinema and Dramatic Literature at the University of North Dakota. He is the author of* Four Great Comedians: Chaplin, Lloyd, Keaton, Langdon *and secretary of
the Society for Cinema Studies.*

FOCUS ON
CHAPLIN

edited by
DONALD W. McCAFFREY

A SPECTRUM BOOK

Prentice-Hall, Inc.
Englewood Cliffs, N.J.

PRENTICE-HALL INTERNATIONAL, INC. (*London*)
PRENTICE-HALL OF AUSTRALIA, PTY. LTD. (*Sydney*)
PRENTICE-HALL OF CANADA, LTD. (*Toronto*)
PRENTICE-HALL OF INDIA PRIVATE LIMITED (*New Delhi*)
PRENTICE-HALL OF JAPAN, INC. (*Tokyo*)

for
my girls,
Marcie, Connie, Jo-Jo,
and
my wife,
Joann

CONTENTS

ESSAYS

REVIEWS

PREFACE

I would like to express my appreciation for the services given by those persons connected with the Inter-Library Loan and the Faculty Research Grant Committee of the University of North Dakota for past and present assistance. Suggestions and inspiration for portions of the book were given by Dr. Harry M. Geduld and Timothy J. Lyons. Also, I thank Michael Graham for special help with the illustrations, and my wife, Joann, who has made outstanding contributions to this study and similar projects in the past.

FOCUS ON

CHAPLIN

Introduction
by DONALD W. McCAFFREY

The importance of Charlie Chaplin as an actor and director could be measured by the great number of books and articles that have been devoted to his life and works. Chaplin's films are still being shown and appreciated. Critical and popular success, even when contrary opinions were prevalent, made Chaplin the favorite of cinema audiences for about two-thirds of his forty-year-long screen career. His rivals during the silent age—Harold Lloyd, Buster Keaton, and Harry Langdon—were never as successful in the thirties as Chaplin. Defiantly he produced two silent films, *City Lights* (1931) and *Modern Times* (1936), when all the other comedians had turned to talkies. His prestige and skills still blossomed when he turned to sound in 1940 with *The Great Dictator*.

An accurate picture of this artist can only be realized by surveying his development from the beginning of his screen career. As an actor-director Chaplin served an apprenticeship with Mack Sennett for only one year. But that year, 1914, was a fervent, frenzied period for the Keystone Film Company. In twelve months Chaplin appeared in thirty-four short works and one feature; he directed (and usually wrote) twenty one- or two-reel films. In the process of this fevered creativity for the Sennett company, the comedian developed the basis of his art. Not one of these Keystone creations ranks with his best works, but it was a formative period—a necessary step in the comedian's evolving grasp of the cinema medium.

Though still in an embryonic state, Chaplin's talents as an actor-director began to emerge when he left Sennett in 1915. As he worked for Essanay, his fame spread so much in one year that he was allowed more control of the total production of his films. From such simple little two-reelers as *The Tramp* and *The Bank* evolved the character that would become the great comic portrait of all times. Mutual, impressed by his high box office appeal, lured him with more money to its studios. In 1916 through 1917 Chaplin entered another phase of his artistic development. He perfected the two-reel comedy with

1

tighter stories and moved each sequence to more effective dramatic climaxes. Chaplin's skill as an actor also took a sharp turn upward. Then his productivity slowed to a few works a year as he searched for a new mode and new materials. He needed a larger canvas.

After five short works for First National, Chaplin took the final step: he moved to the feature length film with *The Kid* in 1921. The richness of his character portrayal sprang forth. A greater range of humor was finally achieved because the feature allowed the actor-director-writer the total dimension of the Little Tramp. While his two-reelers often moved in the rapid, farcical, slapstick style of Mack Sennett, his features explored the spectrum of his little tramp-clown. The quiet, personal moments of the little social outcast evolved, and what critics called "Chaplin's pathos" was born.

With four more silent features, *The Gold Rush* (1925), *The Circus* (1928), *City Lights* (1931), and *Modern Times* (1936) Chaplin reached the zenith of his creative abilities. The tramp-clown figure was the center, the focus, of his creation. Such famous people as stage actress Minnie Maddern Fiske had recognized his genius in 1916. By the thirties critics of the theater such as Brooks Atkinson, Stark Young, and George Jean Nathan turned temporarily from stage drama to cinema to discuss the phenomenon, Charlie Chaplin.

Because his fame as a star was so widespread and his talents as a director-writer so formidable, the comedian's creations were often thought to be the production of a self-made man and a genius. But Chaplin was a product of a great comic film milieu. Harold Lloyd, Buster Keaton, Harry Langdon, and many minor comedians directly and indirectly influenced his work. Furthermore, as Jack Spears points out, Chaplin owed a great deal to Mack Sennett and Mabel Normand in his formative years and to the assistance later of such talents as Monta Bell, Harry d'Abbadie d'Arrast, A. Edward Sutherland, Charles F. Riesner, Robert Aldrich, and Robert Florey.[1] The contributions of these men as assistant directors, advisers, and writers will never be fully realized. Chaplin employed the working method of most major comedians of the twenties (such as Lloyd and Keaton) by demanding full control of all phases of film production from inception to the release of the movie.

Ironically, the famous comedian's artistic decline was seeded when he burlesqued the machine age with *Modern Times* in 1936. By that time Chaplin had become a victim of a routine, mechanical system of motion picture production. An article in *The Literary Digest* pin-pointed the change in his working methods:

[1] Jack Spears, "Chaplin Collaborators," *Films in Review*, January 1962, pp. 18–36.

In the past, he has "shot off the cuff," improvising as he went along, advancing the plot as notions came to him. . . . He made it [*Modern Times*] from a prepared scenario, discovering almost at once that costs would rise beyond good sense if he relied on the old improvisation.[2]

Although modern production techniques seemed to stifle the "free spirit" and the artistic grace of the comedian, he continued with works that were strong even though they often lacked the brilliance of his early silent screen works. An overall stiffness or self-consciousness permeated the sound films *The Great Dictator* (1940), *Monsieur Verdoux* (1947), and *Limelight* (1952). Part of the rigidity of these pictures can be explained by Chaplin's tendency to turn his back on the technical developments in the medium. He never embraced the full potentials of sound, editing, and the moving camera.[3] But even in decline Chaplin's genius radiated a charm that make his last works fascinating films. When popular success waned in the forties and fifties, the comedian still had his defenders. Even when it became popular to berate him for his last efforts, those who witnessed reruns of his earlier works and who could remember the gold mine of films he had given the world, praised his contribution to the screen.

So much has been written on Chaplin's artistic gifts and his place in the sun (as if some critics were his press agents)—it becomes difficult to evaluate his contribution to film art. Concluding a review of the comedian's *My Autobiography* in *Films and Filming,* December 1964 Peter Cotes writes:

Looking back over Chaplin's legendary career as actor, director, producer, musician and screen-writer, and his creation of Charlie, the world's greatest comedian, the best known figure of our day, and an art which ranged from the pinnacles of high comedy to the ocean depths of human despair, I would call him the First Artist of modern times.[4]

This praise of Chaplin started as early as 1915 and continued

[2] "Chaplin: Machine-Age Don Quixote," *The Literary Digest* 120 (November 2, 1935): 26.

[3] Charles Chaplin, *My Autobiography* (New York: Simon and Schuster, 1964), p. 245. (Also check Richard Meryman's interview of Chaplin in *Life* 67 [March 10, 1967]: 84 and 88.)

[4] Reprinted in Appendix C of Peter Cotes's and Thelma Niklaus's *The Little Fellow; The Life and Work of Charles Spencer Chaplin* (New York: The Citadel Press, 1965), p. 176.

into the forties and fifties. Theodore Huff calls him "a clown in direct descent from the *commedia dell' arte* . . . the twentieth-century counterpart of Arlequin and Grimaldi . . . a symbol of the age, the twentieth-century Everyman." [5] Peter Cotes and Thelma Niklaus emphasize that which they believe to be social significance in the works of the comedian: "He and Dickens are of the same stock, filled with the same humanism, the same passionate pity for the underdog, the same blaze of anger against persecution, exploitation, and injustice." [6] Robert Payne becomes more rhapsodic in *The Great God Pan; A Biography of the Tramp played by Charles Chaplin* by referring to the character created as Sir Galahad as well as Pan. This dual nature of Chaplain's portrait is seen by Parker Tyler as a "curious compound of Don Quixote and his servant, Sancho Panza" in *City Lights*.[7] His genius has been compared to that of the poets Keats and Byron. Critics have seen Chaplin's art in its relationship to dance and have described him as a Nijinsky. The desire to explain fully the comedian's unique, universal comic character and his artistic genius has pushed some evaluators to strange lengths.

These impressions of Chaplin still exist today, but a more sober, detached attitude toward his work has developed. Isabel Quigly theorizes that this tendency to see Chaplin as unequaled and transcendental is part of the legend that evolved with the great popularity of the character—a fictional being with universal appeal.[8] David Robinson notes the decline in the comedian's critical reputation. He sees this partly as a reaction to the adulation he received in the thirties and forties and to "his simple philosophies" that are "out of key with the times." [9]

Although critics now see Chaplin as part of the total milieu of his age (crediting Keaton particularly with outstanding contributions to the art of film comedy), they still rate him first because of the range of his portrait and the universality of his humor. The creator of the Little Tramp realized how much the public desired Charlie when he released *Monsieur Verdoux*: " 'I lost money on that one,' he said. 'The people who came to see me came to see the funny man. They were shocked. They couldn't adjust. They

[5] Theodore Huff, *Charlie Chaplin* (New York: Henry Schuman, 1951), p. 1.

[6] Cotes and Nicklaus, p. 13.

[7] Parker Tyler, *Magic and Myth of the Movies* (New York: Henry Holt, 1947), p. 38.

[8] Isabel Quigly, *Charlie Chaplin; Early Comedies* (London: Studio Vista, 1968), pp. 7–12.

[9] David Robinson, *The Great Funnies; A History of Film Comedy* (London: Studio Vista, 1969), p. 69.

wanted to know where the big shoes were.' " [10] *Monsieur Verdoux*
was more favorably received in Europe where it won the Danish
equivalent of an Oscar. Nevertheless, the Charlie of the past was
gone, and the public (and critics) resented the change.

The phenomenon of Charlie probably made one strong contribution that is not fully realized. The adulation of him, as excessive
as it once might have been, helped elevate screen comedy. Too
often comedy drama, on the stage and screen, has been considered a
poor relative of the serious work. Furthermore, Chaplin himself
elevated the often labeled "lowly" slapstick to what some critics
call "high art." Stark Young, however, maintained such a snob
attitude in favor of the serious drama that he wrote the famous
"Dear Mr. Chaplin" article in which he urged Chaplin to under-
take loftier enterprises such as *Liliom, He Who Gets Slapped,* and
Peer Gynt, all stage dramas that Young thought more worthy of the
actor's talents.[11] Fortunately Chaplin did not take the critic's advice
and went on to create his masterpiece, *The Gold Rush,* in 1925.
Certainly, the elevation of raw, slapstick comedy to an art form was a
happy result of Chaplin's genius, but the enthusiastic critical reaction of the time also boosted the status of comedy drama in general.

This study, which features a series of writings that focus on
Chaplin the creator, starts with John Montgomery's history of his
life and works, and then turns to a seldom read personal account
by Chaplin of his work on the stage and with Mack Sennett in the
early Keystone period. Since the comedian only occasionally discussed his working methods in such accounts as *Charlie Chaplin's
Own Story,* the next section features a collection of articles and
evaluations, both Chaplin's own views and those of outside observers, that show the historical development of his theory and techniques of directing and acting. Although the development of film
scholarship has brought more of this type of material to light (such
as Kevin Brownlow's *The Parade's Gone By* . . . which includes
Eddie Sutherland's view of Chaplin's direction in the silent period
and Gloria Swanson's observations on his direction of *A Countess
from Hong Kong* in 1966), I believe that some of the less accessible
articles on the comedian's working method may hold a particular
fascination for interested readers. Consequently, stress is placed on
the early material that is often not available in libraries with a
limited collection of film books and periodicals.

The next three parts of this book form the core of the study.

[10] Interview by unnamed reporter in *The New Yorker* 26 (February 25, 1950): 25.
[11] Stark Young, "Dear Mr. Chaplin," *New Republic* 31 (August 23, 1922): 358.

Evaluations of Chaplin's works have ranged from rhapsodic, impressionistic accounts of the films (such as Louis Delluc's) to detailed studies of scenarios prepared during close viewing of the final creative product—the movie itself. Certain major works (such as Theodore Huff's thorough, well researched examination of Chaplin's life and works and Robert Payne's *The Great God Pan*, an incisive view of the tramp-clown created by the comedian) should be obtained by those interested in film study. Relatively short, overall views of Chaplin's films and of his worth as an artist have been reprinted both to indicate the range of critical opinion through history and to show some of the approaches to analyzing the comedian's contribution to film. A balance of affirmative (Mrs. Fiske and Winston Churchill) and negative (Harcourt Farmer and George Jean Nathan) attitudes toward Chaplin's films in these essays reveals a pattern of pro and con criticism that has existed since the beginning of the comedian's career. I have included an excerpt from my *Four Great Comedians* to illustrate a recent, more "objective" approach to Chaplin's work.

Reviews and evaluations of specific films also reveal the variety of critical opinions and the many ways of evaluating Chaplin's films. This body of film reviews, comparative evaluations, and reflections contains casual as well as literary and scholarly analyses. By showing such various approaches I hope to mirror the total picture of criticism. No one form of evaluation, it is hoped, has been slighted or given undue emphasis. Many of the reviews in this section are advanced to illustrate reactions to the film when it was first released. Francis Hackett, Robert Sherwood, Charles Wood, Alexander Bakshy, and Herman Weinberg are articles of this nature. Reflective evaluations by Timothy Lyons, Gerald Mast, Donald McCaffrey, and Roger Manvell show some of the trends of modern scholarship. Walter Kerr, dramatic critic for the *New York Times,* in "The Lineage of *Limelight*" concludes this section by illustrating a type of analysis that ranges somewhere between the scholarly and journalistic approach. This appraisal assists in summing up Chaplin's bout with the sound comedy film.

This volume focuses on Chaplin the artist and not Chaplin the man. Restrictions in both scope and space make it impossible to examine what might be called "the man and controversy." [12] It can be argued with validity that some of the comedian's works were affected by

---

[12] Views on the personal difficulties of the comedian can be found in such articles as Charles Beaumont's "Chaplin," *Playboy,* March 1960, pp. 81–89; and Terry Hickey's "Accusations against Charles Chaplin for Political and Moral Offenses," *Film Comment,* Winter 1969, pp. 44–56.

public and political harassment—especially *Monsieur Verdoux* (1947) and *A King in New York* (1957)—but the body of his films does not show, or rises above, the taint of reaction to harsh treatment by a fickle public. It should be realized that the comedian's place in history will stand on his works—the films that will live beyond any personal problems that plagued him.

CAREER

A Brief Overall View
by JOHN MONTGOMERY

Of all the comedians whom Mack Sennett discovered for the screen, none became more famous than Charles Chaplin, the little clown with the curly hair, the baggy trousers, the bowler hat, the small mustache, the cane, and the decrepit outsize boots. This was the man described in later years by George Bernard Shaw as "the only genius developed in motion pictures."

He was twenty-six when he joined Sennett, taking with him many of the ideas and traditions of Fred Karno's music-hall troupe, with whom he had gone to America. Ever since then he has faced criticism as well as applause. Some have alleged that even his make-up was stolen from another comedian, Billie Ritchie. Others claim that Billie Ritchie stole Chaplin's ideas. As we now know, Max Linder influenced Chaplin's early technique. Yet it was unmistakably Chaplin himself who made his own personal triumph, and because success usually brings with it responsibilities and the fierce spotlight of public opinion, this man, more than anyone else in Hollywood, has been constantly under fire. There are more fools in the world than Chaplin has portrayed.

He was born on April 16, 1889, if one is to believe a relative, at 287 Kennington Road, London. But according to author Thomas Burke, he was born in Chester Street, which runs between Kennington Road and Lower Kennington Lane. The American *Picture Play* magazine for April 1916 announced that he was not born in London at all, but in Paris. Chaplin himself has agreed that he may

From Comedy Films *by John Montgomery (London: George Allen & Unwin Ltd., 1954), pp. 97–117. Reprinted by permission of the publisher. This account, excerpted from chapter seven, "Chaplin—The Perfect Clown," does not include the productions* Limelight (1952), A King in New York (1957), *or* A Countess from Hong Kong (1966), *but the quintessence of Chaplin's work existed before this final period, which was a time of decline.*

11

have been born in Paris, and not London. But it matters little where or when he made his debut, for as we shall see, his appeal soon became international, and his contribution to the comedy of all nations is now historic.

The son of a singer and a dancer, young Charles had to contribute towards keeping the family when his father died. His mother, who had twice before been married, danced by day, and at night earned extra money by dressmaking. They lived in a poor but neat house, and although he was later to know great wealth and security, young Charles never forgot his early days, and the struggle for the necessities of life.

When he was ten he was on the music halls, already old in ideas, having sung at smoking concerts and in public houses. He was a good clog dancer, and was learning to be a mimic, but for all his juvenile ability the pay was poor, and his first shillings did little to swell the family budget. When he was seven he had nearly been drowned through falling into the Thames from the steps at Westminster Bridge, and soon after this he had made his film debut by posing himself in front of a newsreel camera which was filming the Scots Guards marching through St. James's Park.

In 1905 he won his first important stage role, playing Billy, the boy assistant to Sherlock Holmes, in the London production of *Sherlock Holmes* with William Gillette and Irene Vanbrugh. Backstage, young Chaplin talked to Arthur Conan Doyle, and it was jokingly agreed that in future each would share the earnings of the other. Later Gillette added a curtain raiser called *The Painful Predicament of Sherlock Holmes* to the play *Clarice*, and Chaplin again played the part of Billy, opening at the Duke of York's theater on October 3, 1905.

When the play closed he was out of work, and was forced by circumstances to accept an engagement in an East End music hall as "Sam Cohen, the Jewish comedian." He was not much of a success, and soon afterwards he started a twelve months' engagement at forty-five shillings a week, appearing in a juvenile sketch combination in *Casey's Court Circus*, in which he impersonated the celebrated showman "Doctor" Walford Bodie. Here he was so successful that he joined his half-brother Sidney as a member of Fred Karno's dumb-show comedy company, playing among other roles the part of the drunken swell in *Mumming Birds*, a comedy sketch which was known later in America as *A Night in an English Music Hall*. Others had played the part before him, including Billie Ritchie.

With Karno he learned the hard way, traveling all over Britain and going twice to America. The repertoire was varied; there were sketches about drunks, thieves, family relations, billiards champions, boxers, Turkish baths, policemen, singers who prepared to sing but somehow never started, conjurers who spoiled their own tricks, and pianists who lost the music . . . a wide variety of subjects, mixed with a little honest vulgarity.

In later years Chaplin admitted that it was not always easy to make people laugh. "The mere fact of a hat being blown off isn't funny," he explained. "What is funny is to see its owner running after it, with his hair blowing about, and his coat tails flying. A man walking down a street—that isn't funny. But placed in a ridiculous and embarrassing position the human being becomes a source of laughter to his fellow creatures."

In *Mumming Birds* Chaplin learned many of the tricks which he later introduced on the screen. He was by no means the only comedian in the show, or the one who always got the most laughs. There was another boy who also did well, and whom many people thought equally funny. His role was that of a boy in an Eton collar who fell out of the stage box in excitement. And his name was Stan Laurel.

Chaplin was playing in *A Night in an English Music Hall* in Philadelphia, during his second visit to America, when he received the telegram which was to alter his life:

ARE YOU THE MAN WHO PLAYED THE DRUNK IN THE BOX IN THE ORPHEUM THEATER THREE YEARS AGO STOP IF SO WILL YOU GET IN TOUCH WITH KESSEL AND BAUMANN LONGACRE BUILDING NEW YORK
MACK SENNETT.

Chaplin went to see Kessel and Baumann, the owners of Keystone, and was slightly surprised to receive an offer to go into pictures. He thought the matter over, and paid a visit to one or two picture theaters. What he saw did not convince him that he should abandon his stage career, but he realized that at some time in the future the screen might offer him better opportunities than the music halls.

"I hate to leave the troupe," he said. "How do I know that pictures are going to be a successful medium for pantomime? Suppose I don't make good? I'll be stranded in a strange country." Nevertheless, he accepted 150 dollars a week for a year's trial contract, and joined Mabel Normand, Ford Sterling, Arbuckle, and the other popular Keystone comics, making his debut in 1913 as a reporter in *Making a Living*, with Virginia Kirtley, Henry Lehrman, and Alice Davenport. Afterwards he was teamed for the first time with Mabel Normand in *Mabel's Strange Predicament*.

At first Chaplin's humor did not appeal to Sennett, who was afterwards said to have offered him money to cancel his contract. Chaplin refused, and continued to share a dressing room with Arbuckle, Mack Swain, and two other comedians. They took very little notice of the Englishman, whose first appearances on the screen were made not in his now famous disguise, but with a drooping mustache, ordinary shoes, and a battered top hat. Chaplin's personality was at first used only to carry out Sennett's comedy ideas. Most of his individual comedy was lost in the speed of each film, and in such pictures as *Cruel, Cruel Love* and *Caught in a Cabaret,* to name only two, he had little chance to prove his ability. It was not until he adopted the role of a seedy dandy—as portrayed by Max Linder in some of his French comedies—and later borrowed an old pair of Ford Sterling's shoes to accentuate a comedy walk, together with a pair of Arbuckle's wide baggy pants, that he began to shine. Then it was the public which picked him out from the galaxy of comics, demanding to know who he was, and asking for more.

Sennett wisely decided to give them more, and suggested to Chaplin that he should play a larger part, supporting Marie Dressler in Keystone's six-reel comedy, *Tillie's Punctured Romance.* The cast was to be as follows:

Tillie, the Farmer's Daughter	Marie Dressler
The City Slicker	Charlie Chaplin
The City Girl Friend	Mabel Normand
Tillie's Father	Mack Swain
Café Owner	Edgar Kennedy
Film Actress	Minta Durfee
Detective	Charlie Murray
Detective	Charlie Chase
Society Guest	Harry McCoy
Society Guest	Chester Conklin

As one of the two Society Guests, Harry McCoy was made up to look exactly like Ford Sterling. It is a common error to suppose that Sterling appeared in this film, and his name is usually included in cast lists. But actually he had left Keystone before the picture was made. The Keystone cops included Slim Summerville, Hank Mann, and Eddie Sutherland, and the part of a film actress was played by Arbuckle's wife, Minta Durfee, who is usually left out of the cast lists.

In America the picture established Chaplin as a leading comedian. In Britain it was not released until 1916, by which time his subsequent Essanay films were being shown. He played the part of a smart man about town, dressed in natty suiting and sporting a thin penciled mustache with a break in the middle. The toothbrush mustache which he had worn in earlier pictures was temporarily abandoned.

The film showed Chaplin in an unsympathetic light, and it ended with Marie Dressler chasing him and Mabel Normand, with the aid of the cops, in motorboats and rowing boats. Finally, Marie Dressler ended up in the sea.

In April 1915, when London children were singing "When the Moon Shines Bright on Charlie Chaplin," the *New York Herald* was able to report that "The Chaplin craze seems to have supplanted the Pickford craze," and in this year the comedian left Mack Sennett to join the Essanay company. Once Chaplin had gone, Sennett realized that the old films in which he had appeared were now valuable. Pictures in which he had made only a fleeting appearance were reissued over and over again, often with new titles, until they were worn out. According to E. W. and M. M. Robson, in their book *The Film Answers Back*, one cinema in New York, the Crystal Hall on 14th Street, played nothing but Chaplin pictures for ten years, from 1913 to 1923. There was a break for one week, when one of his best imitators was substituted as an experiment, but business was poor. Next week, when a Chaplin comedy was announced, the patrons returned. It has been estimated that over twenty-five million dollars were paid into the cinemas of the world up to 1921, just to see Chaplin's short films.

In his year with Keystone he had appeared in thirty-five films, produced at the rate of about one a week, except for the six-reeler, which had taken fourteen weeks to complete. Most of these pictures reappeared under fresh titles, to confound the public. Thus when *Making a Living* had been widely shown it was reissued as *A Busted Johnny*, *Troubles*, and *Doing his Best*. *A Film Johnnie* became *Movie Nut* and *Million Dollar Job*. *Caught in a Cabaret* was renamed *The Waiter*, *The Jazz Waiter*, and *Faking with Society*, while *The New Janitor* turned up as *The New Porter* and *The Blundering Boob*. All around the world, over and over again, went the Keystone Chaplins. And they are still showing.

From Essanay Charlie was able to demand 1,250 dollars a week. It is said that Sennett had kept the agents from rival companies away by refusing to allow them near his studio, but that one man—from Essanay—got in disguised as a cowboy "super" and clinched the deal. Not long afterwards Charlie was able to leave Essanay for Mutual, who paid him the princely salary of 10,000 dollars a week, plus a cash bonus of 150,000 dollars.

Back on the Keystone lot he was succeeded by cross-eyed Ben Turpin, who now appeared in dozens of Sennett's films. Unlike many other comics of the time, Turpin did not copy Chaplin. But to be "like Charlie Chaplin" was to ensure success, and few companies did not possess an imitator. Before he donned his famous horn-rimmed

glasses and developed his own style, Harold Lloyd was for a time in
the "Chaplin school." Foremost among the many imitators was Billy
West, appearing in King Bee Comedies with Oliver (Babe) Hardy.
A comedian named Charles Amador became Charles Aplin, and in
1925 Chaplin sued him, and obtained a judgment. France had several
imitators, and in Germany there was a Charlie Kaplin. But Charlie
thrived on imitation, and went from strength to strength, simply because there was nobody quite like him.

The Essanay company gave him more scope than Sennett had done,
and as partners he had Edna Purviance and, before he went to Keystone, Ben Turpin. Charlie was now responsible for more of the actual production, and the laughs were louder. As a boxer with a horseshoe in his glove, or even as a young woman flirting with a middle-
aged man, he kept audiences eagerly asking for more. *His New Job,
The Champion, The Tramp, The Perfect Lady, By the Sea, In the
Park,* and *Police* were all titles which Fred Karno might have given
to his famous music-hall sketches. English humor had conquered the
American screen. The ageless tradition of the clown, the buffoon, the
silent mimic had captured the new medium.

In all he made fourteen films for Essanay, for which he received
some ten times the salary that Sennett had paid him. The old custard-
pie technique was by no means forgotten. There was often a chase,
some drunken stumbling, and comic officialdom to be guyed. There
were gouty feet to be trodden on or caught in revolving doors, some
heavily bearded villains to leer at the beauties, and plenty of action
with the cane, which was useful for balancing, and for moving
drunken bodies out of the path. Large jellies and trifles still sailed
through the air. But Chaplin himself was getting a little more serious,
slightly more mature. And more entertaining.

Not that he ever wanted to play Hamlet. But it was probably
Carmen, his burlesque of the opera, which made him think of making
a more serious type of picture, in which the laughs could be balanced
with the tears, the light tempered with the shade. The Essanay company, however, would not consider his suggestion. They were making
too much money out of laughs to risk losing any on tears. So Charlie
decided to wait.

But from this time onwards he slowed up the knockabout, and began to develop into a player with a purpose behind everything he did.
Although he would always point his moral with the aid of comedy,
his pictures were never again made solely to make people laugh. In
most of them there were to be tears, in some of them slight bitterness.
The tramp who emerged from the slap-happy studio at Edendale was
not an Englishman or an American. His theme was universal, as was
his appeal. It was, and still is, as readily understood in Cairo or Tokyo

as in Boston or Maine. Fundamentally, the peoples of the world are very much alike. And Chaplin knew this, because he was and is at heart an international clown, an entertainer capable of catching the hopes and fears, the sorrows and joys, of the ordinary person, sometimes with only a gesture, the movement of a hand, or the shuffle of his feet. That is the true clown's art.

In May 1915 *The Bioscope* film trade paper reported in Britain that "so strong is the grip of the Chaplin comedies that last week numerous halls in the Liverpool district adopted the expediency of giving special performances, at which the films exhibited consisted exclusively of the Chaplin productions."

In 1916 he left Essanay to join Mutual, for whom his first picture was *The Floorwalker,* with Edna Purviance. In all his Mutual films, and in those which came later, he appeared as a little man who might have come from any city, in any country. In *The Immigrant* he depicted a number of homeless people of different nationalities traveling to America in the steerage of a liner. He showed the Statue of Liberty in the background, and in the next scene depicted the passengers being ruthlessly herded together behind ropes. It was laughable, but it was also an expression of social conditions. Chaplin had started his crusade.

The Mutual pictures included *The Fireman, The Vagabond, One A.M., The Count, The Pawnshop, Behind the Screen, Easy Street, The Cure,* and *The Adventurer.* Many of these were based on familiar themes. *The Rink* was similar to Max Linder's skating film, although there must be a limit to the amount of antics that can be accomplished on skates. In *The Pawnshop* there were two hilarious minutes in which Chaplin passed dishes through a clothes wringer to dry them, then dried a cup in the same way, and finally his hands.

The modern generation rarely sees an early Chaplin film in its original form. Sequences have been cut out, and the original titles lost. The addition of wholly irrelevant commentaries, explaining what Charlie may do next, often spoils the picture. Sound effects are often added, which do nothing to help the comedy. But worst of all is the commentary, all too frequent, which "guys" the classic comedy film, ignoring the fact that the whole picture is being entirely spoiled. In spite of these defects the old Chaplin films are still in great demand, and are likely to remain so as long as people retain their sense of humor. *Easy Street,* considered by many to be the best of the Mutual series, is, with *The Cure,* one of the most popular of all. During 1948, Wallace Heaton, with one of the biggest hiring libraries of substandard films in Britain, kept sixteen copies of *Easy Street* in constant circulation, and did not have a single copy on their shelves.

Late in 1916 Chaplin left Mutual to sign a new contract with the

First National Corporation. The three years with Keystone, Essanay, and Mutual, had established him as the most popular comedian in the world. He was the idol of everybody who could go to the pictures, and in such theaters as the New Gallery Kinema, London—considered to be the smartest picture house in the metropolis—his short comedies were given more prominence than the feature attractions. In the noisier districts of London's Commercial Road, Canning Town, Chingford, and Mile End, the appeal of Chaplin was simply terrific. To Englishmen, and especially to Londoners, he has always been the foremost comedian on the screen, a household name remembered when the name of the last prime minister might be forgotten, the name of the president of France ignored.

In France, during the horrors of the 1914 war, his name was a byword with the troops. Home and beauty were typified by the wife, a hot bath, and Charlie Chaplin—who represented all the gaiety and good feeling of the world to the ordinary Allied soldier. When a Chaplin film arrived at the front it offered entertainment to the troops which few actors could surpass. The officer commanding the Sixth Divisional Supply Column in France wrote to the Essanay company:

Gentlemen,

I have to thank you for your letter of September 11th, forwarded to me today, and for the gift of films. It is impossible to make you realize how much they were appreciated, and I truly wish you could have heard the cheer that went up when Chaplin appeared on the screen. The posters—i.e., cardboard figures of Chaplin, were carried off during the night to the trenches, and have been the subject of great attention by the enemy.

> W. Murphy,
> Major, A.S.C.

By 1917 Chaplin was able to build his own studio—described as a "snug and unobtrusive little affair," and stated to have cost him up to £20,000. It was erected on a site bought for some 30,000 dollars, in the best residential district of Hollywood, a mile away from the existing studio center. The initial ceremony of turning the first earth on his five acres of land was performed by Charlie himself, in the presence of Sid, and a few members of the company. Both brothers took off their coats and began to dig. Then Charlie carted away some earth in a wheelbarrow, and an army of workmen swarmed in.

For the little man from Whitechapel—or was it Paris?—the moment was important. From now on he was relatively independent, working for himself, and at last free to express himself. Under his contract with First National he made eight films, in addition to *The Bond*, which was produced for the Liberty Loan Committee and was issued free. The titles were *A Dog's Life, Shoulder Arms, Sunnyside, A Day's Pleasure, The Kid, The Idle Class, Pay Day*, and *The Pilgrim*. Neither *Sunnyside* nor *A Day's Pleasure* were considered in 1919 to be among Chaplin's best films. His position was by now being contested by the frequent appearance of his rivals Larry Semon, Arbuckle, Harold Lloyd, and Buster Keaton. But with the coming of *The Kid* his supremacy was assured.

Pat Day (1922) was the last two-reeler. Only the less popular comedians were now to be seen exclusively in two-reelers. After this came *The Pilgrim*, in which he was seen as a convict escaping from prison. After exchanging his clothes for those of a parson who was swimming, Charlie walked up the road, only to meet an elderly couple— who asked him to marry them. Escaping to a town, he was greeted warmly by the good folk, who were all collected together to meet the visiting parson. In the pulpit Charlie brilliantly told the story of David and Goliath, entirely in pantomime.

Now that wealth had come his way, he could afford to be generous; 150,000 dollars went to the War Loan, and with Sir Harry Lauder he gave his services for a special short half-reel comedy, the proceeds going to the Loan. He was now making an immense amount of money, and so were the men who marketed and showed his pictures. The British rights in *The Idle Class* (1921) were sold for the record sum of £50,000, but British cinema owners were at first reluctant to pay what they considered high rental charges for the picture.

Shoulder Arms was filmed in 1918, but was not shown in America until three weeks before the armistice. It was felt that the troops might not like the humor, being so familiar with the reality. Five reels had been planned, but they were finally cut down to three. There was really no danger of the troops being offended, and it was generally considered to be Chaplin's best picture. As an awkward recruit unable to stand in line because of his extraordinary feet, Charlie reached new heights of comedy. Every humorous war picture of later years was to be influenced by *Shoulder Arms*. When at last the shouts of his fearful sergeant had died away, the new recruit was seen asleep in the barrack room, fitfully dreaming that he was already in the front-line trenches.

The grim nightmare was comic, yet the settings were realistic and the atmosphere wholly convincing. Charlie's method of opening a bottle was to hold it above the trench until a bullet shattered the top. When every other soldier received his mail from home, he got nothing. But at last his parcel arrived, a cheese so old and ripe that he
package

sought the safety of a gas mask before hurling it far away into the enemy lines.

Peace came at last at the end of the nightmare, with Charlie dreaming that he was sinking to sleep below the water line of a flooded trench, breathing bubbles through a tin funnel. Only a sergeant's head and feet, with a frog sitting on one boot, could be seen above the water level.

Shoulder Arms ended with a sniping expedition into No Man's Land. Disguised as a tree, Charlie was invisible to all but a wandering dog, and when chased up a drainpipe by the enemy, he lost his trousers. Finally came the moment in his dream when he captured the Kaiser, the crown prince, and Von Hindenburg, all at once. Brother Sydney was the Kaiser, but there were objections to this part of the picture, and some cinemas did not show it. The ending was even more sensational, showing the Allied leaders giving a magnificent banquet to Charlie, at which the president of France made a speech. As Charlie rose to reply, the king of England crept up to steal a souvenir button from the hero's coat! Needless to say, the general public did *not* see this sequence.

Shoulder Arms and the other seven films which Chaplin made between 1918 and 1922 for First National represented the fruits of the experience he had gained with Sennett, Essanay, and Mutual, and showed that the comedian was ready for bigger things. In 1920 came *The Kid,* still considered to be one of the outstanding motion pictures of all time. It started melodramatically with the words "Her only sin was motherhood . . ." followed by a scene showing a woman leaving a child on a front doorstep. Then came Charlie the tramp, pausing to remove a fingerless glove, and carefully selecting a cigarette stub from the old sardine tin which he used as a case.

The child star of *The Kid* was Jackie Coogan, and the story continued in a rambling fashion, production being almost on a day-to-day basis, without script or scenario. A dream sequence entitled "Fairyland" showed the tramp and the child in heaven, a happily decorated slum street in which even the policemen flew around with white wings. In order to earn money to keep the boy, the tramp became a glazier, sending the youngster round the houses to break the windows which he could then repair. Later, in *The Gold Rush,* Chaplin provided a variation on this theme by sweeping snow from one house in front of another, then moving on to offer his services at the house where the snow was piled up.

The Kid brought sudden fame to little Jackie Coogan, who had made his stage debut when not quite two by escaping from his father's dressing room clad only in a petticoat, to make an unexpected entrance on the stage. Three years later Chaplin saw him and engaged him for the film. According to tradition, the five-year-old boy winked at the famous comedian in a hotel lobby.

By the time he was ten Coogan had made about £230,000, including £100,000 paid in advance for four future films. When in the autumn of 1924 he went to Greece, he was acclaimed in every country he passed through. American children had subscribed a million dollars to send a mercy cargo of milk and food to the children of Greece, and Jackie Coogan was chosen to deliver it. At Southampton he was received in state by the mayor, and in London enthusiastic crowds greeted him. The harbor of Piraeus, the port of Athens, was beflagged and decorated with hundreds of posters bidding *Zito* (Welcome) to the young ambassador. In Athens he was presented with the Golden Cross of the Order of Jerusalem and the Silver Cross of the Order of George. To the world this boy was Young America, yet within a few years he had slipped from stardom and was no longer even a box-office attraction. When he grew up, people lost interest in him. Of all his many films, *Peck's Bad Boy, Trouble, Oliver Twist,* and *Circus Days,* in which he gave excellent performances, only *The Kid* is remembered. A child star is seldom an adult star. In later years Shirley Temple, Freddie Bartholomew, and for a while Jackie Cooper were to know how hard it is to live down a juvenile reputation, and claim attention as an adult.

Early in 1919 Chaplin joined Mary Pickford, her husband Douglas Fairbanks, and D. W. Griffith, to form the United Artists Corporation. Each was to produce pictures for distribution through their new organization. It was no longer necessary for Chaplin to make many films —certainly not at the rate to which he was accustomed. In future his pictures could be bigger, but less frequent.

It was not until 1921 that Charlie returned to Europe, when he visited England, France, and Germany. In Paris he found a little café, where he had enjoyed coffee some years before, but it was now closed. There could be little time to remember the past, for Chaplin was the man of the moment. When Max Linder told him that people knew him as Charlot, and his brother Sydney as Julot, Chaplin roared with laughter and insisted on being called Charlot all day. Later he had to be rescued by gendarmes from a howling mob of admirers, all shouting, "Vive Charlot!"

In Paris he met Dudley Field Malone, Waldo Francis, and Georges Carpentier, and went to see Versailles with Carpentier and Sir Philip Sassoon. When he attended the French première of *The Kid* he found his box decorated with American and British flags, and afterwards he received the Medal of the Beaux Arts. Back at the Crillon Hotel awaiting his return were Douglas Fairbanks and Mary Pickford, with General Pershing.

In England Chaplin had stayed at Lympne in Kent, with Sir Philip Sassoon. When his host asked him to attend the unveiling of the village war memorial Chaplin had hesitated, thinking that a comedian would be out of place at such a ceremony. Nevertheless, he attended the service, to the great delight of the villagers.

A week was spent in Essex with H. G. Wells, of whose novel *The History of Mr. Polly* Chaplin said, "Some day I am going to do it in pictures." But *Mr. Polly* did not appear on the screen for nearly thirty years, and it was then John Mills and not Chaplin who made it. Charlie, however, was quite right—he would have made an excellent Mr. Polly. It was strange that several of the critics who praised John Mills in the film pointed out that he was almost "Chaplinesque" in certain sequences.

James Barrie, Thomas Burke, and Rebecca West were among the celebrities whom he met with H. G. Wells. He showed them how to play baseball, and discussed with St. John Ervine the possibility of making talking pictures. Chaplin expressed his opinion that speech would spoil the art of pantomime, and that talk was totally unnecessary to films.

When he returned to England from France the plane was held up by fog over the Channel, and was two hours late at Croydon. Sir Philip Sassoon had arranged for Chaplin to meet the Prime Minister, David Lloyd George, and because of the delay Chaplin was rather worried. There was a crowd at the airport, where the police cleared a gangway for Chaplin to reach his car. Directly he was in the car, it started off, but instead of going to the Ritz Hotel, Chaplin found himself nearing the Clapham district. When he asked the driver where they were going the man in front pulled off a false mustache and announced: "I am Castleton Knight. You remember me. You promised to visit my theater. My patrons were all told about it, and they expected you. You didn't keep your promise, so I have kidnapped you."

To have kidnapped Charlie Chaplin, right under the noses of the police at Croydon, was no mean achievement. Castleton Knight was the enterprising manager of the Majestic Theater at Clapham. He had simply driven a large car up to the airport, and had announced to the police that he was collecting Mr. Chaplin. Luckily, Chaplin thought it was a good joke, and at once agreed to appear on the stage of the Majestic. He made a short speech to a delighted audience, and went on in the car to his hotel.

The European visit had started at Southampton, where he had been greeted by the mayor and a civic reception. In his book *My Wonderful Visit,* he later described the welcome at Waterloo Station:

The barriers are broken. They are coming on all sides. Policemen are elbowing and pushing. Girls are shrieking—"Charlie! Charlie! There he is! Good luck to you, Charlie! God bless you!"

He did not like the hysterical adoration of the crowds. And in his first four days in London he received 73,000 letters, of which 671 were from relatives in Britain, of whom he knew nothing. Most of them claimed to be cousins, but nine different women said they were his mother. Almost all the writers asked to be set up in business, to meet him, or to go on the films.

After being introduced by Edward Knoblock to E. V. Lucas, Chaplin accepted an invitation to dinner at the Garrick Club, where he sat next to J. M. Barrie, who suggested that *Peter Pan* ought to be filmed. They continued the discussion in Barrie's flat until three o'clock in the morning.

In Germany Chaplin was almost unknown, for only *The Rink* had been shown there. On his first evening in Berlin he went to a leading restaurant, but, not being in evening clothes, was placed in a corner at a small table, where he sat meekly eating his dinner, with only a poor view of the crowded room. As he was leaving, a man from a more important table jumped up and walked quickly to greet him. It was Alf Kaufman, the European representative of Parmount Pictures, who at once persuaded Chaplin to join his table, where his wife was sitting with Pola Negri.

"Negri is a wonderful person," said Chaplin afterwards. "Young, vivacious, beautiful. She speaks no English—she is Polish, you know, not German, even though she has played in German pictures. We became very good friends, and I dined with the same party every one of the three nights in Berlin. Negri is coming to America in January to make pictures in California. She will be a revelation."

She certainly was a revelation, and so was Ernst Lubitsch, the German director of her films, whom Chaplin also met. But because Lubitsch knew no English, and Chaplin could speak very little German, conversation was difficult.

In an interview with George P. West in 1923 Chaplin revealed that the now familiar tramp outfit helped him to express the conception of the average man, whom he sought to represent on the screen. "The derby (bowler), too small, is striving for dignity," he explained. "The mustache is vanity. The tightly buttoned coat and the stick and his whole manner are a gesture towards gallantry and dash and 'front.' He is trying to meet the world bravely, to put up a bluff, and he knows that, too. He knows it so well that he can laugh at himself, and pity himself a little."

It was in this year that Chaplin decided to realize his ambition and make a serious film. *A Woman of Paris* was the result, an almost tragic story of two young people forbidden to marry. Edna Purviance and Adolphe Menjou were the stars, and Chaplin himself appeared for a brief second, walking almost unnoticed across the screen.

He tried most of his films out "on the dog," as he used to say, arranging to show his latest picture unannounced in a normal cinema program. Then he would sit in the audience and watch, and listen to what people said, and note where they laughed. If they laughed he was happy, but if they did not then he cut out the sequence. There was not very much that he had to cut, once he had completed his film.

In 1925 came *The Gold Rush*, "the picture I want to be remembered by," said Chaplin at the time. The famous log-cabin scenes, together with the dancing fingers and the eating of his boots, are memorable. The picture was the first comedy which he made entirely on his own account, and it took a year to complete, and cost over 800,000 dollars.

It was two years before he made his next, *The Circus*. Whether cooking an egg, being chased into the sawdust ring, or swallowing a horse pill because the horse blew down the tube first—the little man was always in trouble. But the pathos paid handsome dividends, and during its first week of showing in New York 105,000 people paid £14,500 to see the film.

In *The Circus* Chaplin appeared as a man in search of a job. Unknowingly he becomes the accomplice of a pickpocket, and is soon wanted by the police. When a policeman sees him, he runs off to hide in a circus, where he is engaged as an odd-job man. But he is so clumsy that he is dismissed. When the circus men go on strike he is reengaged, and falls in love with the daughter of the owner—a love which he is too shy to reveal.

With the coming of talking films, Chaplin's future hung in the balance. But two years later he decided to challenge the new technique by making a silent comedy with recorded music. This he called *City Lights*, described as a "comedy romance in pantomime." Although in 1930 all Hollywood was making noisy singing and dancing pictures, he decided to keep his film silent, except for an original musical score and sound effects.

When a reporter from a Hollywood magazine asked Chaplin what he thought of sound films, he was reported to have replied: "Talkies? You can say I detest them! They come to ruin the world's most ancient art, the art of pantomime. They annihilate the great beauty of silence."

City Lights probably represents the highest achievements of the silent film, which by 1928 had reached perfection as a method of telling a story without speech. It is the tale of a tramp who falls in love with a blind flower girl. She mistakes him for a wealthy man, and through his devotion regains her sight. Pathos and hilarious knock-about comedy are carefully mixed, the highlights being a night-club sequence in which Chaplin eats spaghetti and streamers, a brilliant dancing boxing match set to music, and a delightful supporting performance by Harry Myers as the millionaire who knows Chaplin only when he is drunk. The boxing match, one of the funniest sequences ever filmed, is timed with masterly precision. It would be impossible to see it without laughing. The final close-up, in which the flower girl (Virginia Cherrill) realizes that the pathetic little tramp is her benefactor, is one of the most poignant of film scenes.

Nineteen years after its first release in Britain, *City Lights* was revived and later generally released to delight a new generation. Silence had indeed proved golden, for the Chaplin of 1930 has proved to be a greater comedian than any of his rivals of 1950. The evidence was contained in a nineteen-year-old film.

"A comedy is only as funny as its gags"—in this one sentence Larry Semon had held the whole key to the success of comic films. And because both Chaplin and Semon were *clowns,* their gags were visual ones. *City Lights,* like every Chaplin film, had plenty. The tramp watches a man walk past him smoking a cigar, jumps into a Rolls-Royce, and follows the wealthy one down the street. When the man throws the cigar end onto the sidewalk, the tramp stops the car and makes for it. But from out of the shadows comes another tramp, who gets there first. Whereupon Charlie dashes up, pushes the intruder over, snatches the cigar end, and drives off in his car. The scene fades out on the dazed intruder, watching with amazement the spectacle of a cigar-butt collector driving around in a Rolls-Royce. When analyzed, every comedy sequence in this film is a gag, or a collection of gags.

In 1935 came *Modern Times,* the story of a worker in the twentieth-century machine age. It was a silent film, except for a gibberish song, sung by Chaplin himself to the tune of "Titina." The message behind *Modern Times* was more obvious than it had been in his previous films. The absurdity of the mechanical era was paraded for everyone to see. The moral behind the laughs was clear, as it was in *The Great Dictator,* which ridiculed not only Hitler and Mussolini, but all dictatorship, in every form. Man's inhumanity to man was clearly shown. And if there was slightly less to laugh at than there had been in *The Cure* and *Easy Street,* this was because by the time the picture was shown dictatorship was hardly a laughing matter, Hitler and Mussolini being at war with half the world.

Monsieur Verdoux, which came some years later, proved to be an even more serious picture. Now that he had talked on the screen, in *The Great Dictator,* it was obvious that his new film would rely greatly on dialogue. But in place of the baggy pants and shabby coat, he now wore the smart morning clothes and silk hat of a French Blue-beard—a murderer who disposed of his wives with finesse. Murder is a strange subject for a jest, and it was not surprising that many members of the public could not readily appreciate the chilly atmos-phere of the new picture. Yet even in this unusual story the bril-liantly polished performance of Chaplin the actor did much to over-come the opposition. He held the screen completely, his timing was a delight, and his diction was as perfect as every gesture that he made.

In America *Monsieur Verdoux* was not a great success. In some states it was boycotted, the Catholic War Veterans and other organiza-tions protested that it was unsocial and unpleasant, and pickets were placed outside the theaters which showed it. The fact that in one scene in the film Chaplin had made a veiled plea for the cause of Christianity was ignored. Sections of the press attacked the picture vigorously. Chaplin's private life, which had claimed the attention of the more scurrilous American newspapers for some years, was again laid bare.

Simply because of the press reports, and what they had heard about it, large sections of the public stayed away from *Monsieur Verdoux*. Many believed that it might be too "highbrow" for them. They could not visualize a Chaplin who did not make them rock with laughter. After all, that is what he had always done in the past. But in Europe the film was more successful, the press being more enthusiastic, and the public, particularly in Britain, being anxious to see Chaplin, what-ever film he had made.

Creating the Role of Doctor Body in
CASEY'S COURT CIRCUS
by CHARLIE CHAPLIN

. . . I consented to become a member of *Casey's Circus*, and returned whistling to our lodgings, able to face Sidney with some degree
of pride because I had an engagement at last.

We began rehearsals next day in a very dirty dark room over a public house—fifteen ragged, hungry-looking, sallow-faced boys desperately being funny under the direction of a fat greasy-looking manager
who smelled strongly of ale. It was difficult work for me at first. Being
funny is at best a hard job, and being funny in those conditions,
which I heartily detested, seemed at first almost impossible. More than
once, when the manager swore at me more than usual, I felt like
throwing the whole thing up and would have done so but for the
dread of going back to the endless tramping up and down the Strand
and being a burden on Sidney.

Casey's Circus was putting on that season a burlesque of persons in
the public eye, and I was cast for the part of Doctor Body, a patent-
medicine faker, who was drawing big crowds on the London street cor-
ners and selling a specific for all the ills of man and beast at a shilling
the bottle. Watching him one afternoon, I was seized with a great
idea. I would let the manager rehearse me all he jolly well liked, but
when the opening night came I would play Doctor Body as he really
was—I would put on such a marvelous character delineation that even
the lowest music-hall audience would recognize it as great acting and
I would be rescued by some good manager and brought back to a
West End theater.

The idea grew upon me. Despising with all my heart the cheap,

From Charlie Chaplin's Own Story (*Indianapolis: Bobbs-Merrill,*
1916), pp. 170–76. Critics in 1916 found this autobiography a mixture
of fact and fiction. Because of embarrassment, the comedian eventu-
ally had the book withdrawn from the market.

clap-trap burlesque which the manager tried to drill into me, I paid only enough attention to it to get through rehearsals somehow, hurrying out afterward to watch Doctor Body and to practise before the mirror in our lodgings my own idea of the part. I felt that I did it well and thrilled with pride at the thought of playing it soon with the eye of a great manager upon me.

The night of the opening came and I hurried to the dirty makeshift dressing room in a cheap East End music hall with all the sensations of a boy committing his first burglary. I must manage to make up as the real Doctor Body and to get on the stage before I was caught. Once on the stage, without the burlesque make-up which I was supposed to wear, I knew I could make the part go. I painted my face stealthily among the uproar and quarrels of the other fourteen boys, who were all in the same dressing room fighting over the mirrors and hurling epithets and make-up boxes at one another.

The air tingled with excitement. The distracted manager, thrusting his head in at the door, cried with oaths that Casey himself was in front and he'd stand for no nonsense. We could hear him rushing away, swearing at the scene shifters, who had made some error in placing the set. The audience was in bad humor; we could faintly hear it hooting and whistling. It had thrown rotten fruit at the act preceding ours. In the confusion I managed to make up and to get into my clothes, troubled by the size of the high hat I was to wear, which came down over my ears. I stuffed it with paper to keep it at the proper angle on my head, and trembling with nervousness, but sure of myself when I should get on the stage, I stole out of the dressing room and stationed myself in the darkest part of the wings.

The boy who appeared first was having a bad time of it, missing his cues and being hissed and hooted by the audience. The manager rushed up to me, caught sight of my make-up and stopped aghast.

" 'Ere, you can't go on like that!" he said in a furious whisper, catching my arm.

"Let me alone; I know what I'm doing!" I cried angrily, wrenching myself from him. My great plan was not to be spoiled now at the last minute. The manager reached for me again, purple with wrath, but, quick as an eel, I ducked under his arm, seized the cane I was to carry and rushed on to the stage half a minute too soon.

Once in the glare of the footlights I dropped into the part, determined to play it, play it well, and hold the audience. The other boy, whose part I had spoiled, confused by my unexpected appearance, stammered in his lines and fell back. I advanced slowly, impressively, feeling the gaze of the crowd, and, with a carefully studied gesture, hung my cane—I held it by the wrong end! Instead of hanging on my arm, as I expected it, it clattered on the stage. Startled, I stooped to pick it up, and my high silk hat fell from my head. I grasped it, put it on quickly, and, paper wadding falling out, I found my whole head buried in its black depths.

A great burst of laughter came from the audience. When, pushing the hat back, I went desperately on with my serious lines, the crowd roared, held its sides, shrieked with mirth till it gasped. The more serious I was, the funnier it struck the audience. I came off at last, pursued by howls of laughter and wild applause, which called me back again. I had made the hit of the evening.

"That was a good bit of business, my lad," Mr. Casey himself said, coming behind the scenes and meeting me in the wings when finally the audience let me leave the stage the second time. "Your idea?"

"Oh, certainly," I replied airily. "Not bad, I flatter myself—er— but of course not what I might do at that." And, seizing the auspicious moment, I demanded a raise of two pounds a week and got it.

The next week I was headlined as "Charles Chaplin, the funniest actor in London," and *Casey's Circus* packed the house wherever it was played. I had stumbled on the secret of being funny—unexpectedly. An idea, going in one direction, meets an opposite idea suddenly. "Ha! Ha!" you shriek. It works every time.

I walk on to the stage, serious, dignified, solemn, pause before an easy chair, spread my coat tails with an elegant gesture—and sit on the cat. Nothing funny about it, really, especially if you consider the feelings of the cat. But you laugh. You laugh because it is unexpected. Those little nervous shocks make you laugh; you can't help it. Peeling onions makes you weep, and seeing a fat man carrying a custard pie slip and sit down on it makes you laugh.

In the two years I was with *Casey's Circus* I gradually gave up my idea of playing great parts on the dramatic stage. I grew to like the comedy work, to enjoy hearing the bursts of laughter from the audience, and getting the crowd in good humor and keeping it so was a nightly frolic for me. Then, too, by degrees all my old self-confidence and pride came back, with the difference, indeed, that I did not take them too seriously, as before, but merely felt them like a pleasant inner warmth as I walked on the Strand and saw the envious looks of other actors not so fortunate.

Acting-Directing Apprenticeship
with Mack Sennett
by CHARLIE CHAPLIN

I reached Los Angeles late at night, very glad that I would not have to report at the Keystone studios until morning. I tried to oversleep next day, but it was impossible; I was awake long before dawn. I dressed as slowly as possible, wandered about the streets as long as I could, and finally ordered an enormous breakfast, choosing the most expensive café I could find, because the more expensive the place the longer one must wait to be served, and I was seizing every pretext for delay. When the food came I could not eat it, and suddenly I said to myself that I was behaving like a child; I would hurry to the studios and get it over. I rushed from the café, called a taxi, and bribed the chauffeur to break the speed laws and get me there quick.

When I alighted before the studio, a big new building of bright unpainted wood, I took a deep breath, gripped my cane firmly, walked briskly to the door—and hurried past it. I walked a block or so, calling myself names, before I could bring myself to turn and come back. At last, with the feeling that I was dragging myself by the collar, I managed to get up the steps and push open the door.

I was welcomed with a cordiality that restored a little of my self-confidence. The director of the company in which I was to star had been informed of my arrival by telegraph and was waiting for me on the stage, they said. An office boy, whistling cheerfully, volunteered to take me to him, and, leading me through the busy offices, opened the stage door.

A glare of light and heat burst upon me. The stage, a yellow board floor covering at least two blocks, lay in a blaze of sunlight, intensified by dozens of white canvas reflectors stretched overhead. On it

From Charlie Chaplin's Own Story (*Indianapolis: Bobbs-Merrill,* *1916), pp. 198–231.*

was a wilderness of "sets"—drawing rooms, prison interiors, laundries, balconies, staircases, caves, fire escapes, kitchens, cellars. Hundreds of actors were strolling about in costume; carpenters were hammering away at new sets; five companies were playing before five clicking cameras. There was a roar of confused sound—screams, laughs, an explosion, shouted commands, pounding, whistling, the bark of a dog. The air was thick with the smell of new lumber in the sun, flashlight powder, cigarette smoke.

The director was standing in his shirt-sleeves beside a clicking camera, holding a mass of manuscript in his hand and clenching an unlighted cigar between his teeth. He was barking short commands to the company which was playing—"To the left; to the left, Jim! There, hold it! Smile, Maggie! That's right. Good! Look out for the lamp!"

The scene over, he welcomed me cordially enough, but hurriedly. "Glad to see you. How soon can you go to work? This afternoon? Good! Two o'clock, if you can make it. Look around the studio a bit, if you like. Sorry I haven't a minute to spare; I'm six hundred feet short this week, and they're waiting for the film. G'by. Two o'clock, sharp!" Then he turned away and cried, "All ready for the next scene. Basement interior," and was hard at work again.

The little self-confidence I had been able to muster failed me entirely when the director dismissed me so crisply. The place was so strange to my experience, every one of the hundreds of persons about me was so absorbed in his work, barely glancing at me as I passed, that I felt helpless and out of place there. Still, the studio was crowded with interesting things to see, and I determined to remain and learn all I could of this novel business of producing cinema film before my own turn came to do it. So I assumed an air of dignity, marred somewhat by the fact that my collar was beginning to wilt and my nose burning red in the hot sunlight, and strolled down the stage behind the clicking cameras.

At a little distance I saw the front of a three-story tenement, built of brick, with windows and fire escape all complete, looking quite natural in front, but supported by wooden scaffolding behind. Near it, on a high platform, was a big camera, and a man with a shade over his eyes busy adjusting it, and a dozen men were stretching a net such as acrobats use. A number of actors were hurrying in that direction, and I joined them, eager to see what was to happen.

"What's all the row?" I asked a girl in the costume of a nurse, who stood eating a sandwich, the only idle person in sight.

"Scene in a new comedy," she answered pleasantly but indifferently.

"Ah, yes. That's in my own line," I said importantly. "I am Charles Chaplin."

She looked at me, and I saw that she had never heard of me.

"You're a comedian?" she inquired.

"Yes," I answered sharply. "Er—do you go on in this?"

"Oh, no. I'm not an actress," she said, surprised. "I'm here professionally." I did not understand what she meant. "In case of acacidents," she explained, plainly thinking me stupid. "Sometimes nothing happens, but you never can tell. Eight men were pretty badly hurt in the explosion in the comedy they put on last week," she finished brightly.

I felt a cold sensation creep up my spine.

In the "set" before us there was a great bustle of preparation. A long light ladder was set up at a sharp angle, firmly fastened at the bottom, but with the upper end unsupported, quivering in the air.

Men were running about shouting directions and questions. Suddenly, balancing precariously on the narrow platform behind the camera operator, the director appeared and clapped his hands sharply. "All ready down there?" he called.

"All ready!" some one yelled in reply.

"Let 'er go!"

The windows in the brick wall burst outward with a loud explosion and swirling clouds of smoke. Up the swaying ladder ran a policeman and at the same instant, caught up by invisible wires, another man soared through the air and met him. On the top rung of the ladder they balanced, clutching each other.

"Fight! Fight! Put some life into it!" yelled the director. "Turn on the water, Jim!"

My eyes straining in their sockets, I saw the two men in the air slugging each other desperately, while the ladder bent beneath them. Then from the ground a two-inch stream of water rose and struck them—held there, playing on them while they struggled.

"Great! Great! Keep it up!" the director howled. "More smoke!" Another explosion answered him; through the eddying smoke I could see the two men still fighting, while the stream from the hose played on them.

"Let go now. Fall! Fall! I tell you, fall!" the director shouted. The two men lurched, the wires gave way, and, falling backward, sheer, from a height of twenty-five feet, the comedian dropped and struck the net. The net broke.

The scene broke up in a panic. The nurse ran through the crowd, a stretcher appeared, and on it the comedian was carried past me, followed by the troubled director and a physician. "Not serious, merely shock; he'll be all right tomorrow," the physician was saying, but I felt my knees shaking under me.

"So *this* is the life of a cinema comedian!" I thought, breathing hard.

I did not feel hungry, some way, and besides, I felt that if I left the studio for luncheon I would probably be unable to bring myself back again, so I picked out the coolest place I could find and sat down to await two o'clock. I was in a dim damp "basement set," furnished only with an overturned box, on which I sat. After a time a strange scratching noise attracted my attention, and looking down I saw a procession of bright red and blue rats coming out between my feet. I leaped from the box with my hair on end and left, saying nothing to anyone.

At two o'clock, quivering with nervousness, I presented myself to the director. He was brisk and hurried as before and plunged immediately into a description of the part I was to play, pausing only to mop his perspiring forehead now and then. The heat had increased; under the reflectors the place was like a furnace, but my spine was still cold with apprehension.

"Is it an acrobatic part?" I asked, as soon as I could force myself to inquire.

"No, not this one. You're a hungry tramp in the country. We'll take the interiors here, and for the rest we'll go out on 'location,' " the director answered, ruffling the pages of the "working script" of the play. "We'll do the last scene first—basement set. Let's run through it now; then you can make up and we'll get it on the film before the light's gone."

He led the way to the basement set and began to instruct me how to play the part.

"You fall in, down the trap door," he said. "Pick yourself up, slowly, and register surprise. Don't look at the camera, of course. You have a pie under your coat. Take it out, begin to eat it. Register extreme hunger. Then you hear a noise, start, set down the pie, and peer out through the grating. When you turn around the rats will be eating the pie. Get it?"

I said I did, and while the director peered through the camera lens I rehearsed as well as I could. I had to do it over and over, because each time I forgot and got out of the range of the camera lens. At last, however, with the aid of a five-foot circle of dots on the floor, I did it passably well, and was sent to make up in one of dozens of dressing rooms, built in a long row beside the stage. My costume, supplied by the Keystone wardrobe, was ready, and I was reassured by the sight of it and the make-up box. Here at last was something I was quite familiar with, and I produced a make-up of which I was proud.

When I returned to the stage the camera operator was waiting, and a small crowd of actors and carpenters had gathered to watch the scene. The director was inspecting the colored rats and giving orders to have their tails repainted—quick, because the blamed things had licked the color off and would register tailless. A stage hand was standing by with a large pie in his hand.

"Ready, Chaplin?" the director called, and then he looked at me.

"Holy Moses, where did you get that make-up?" he asked in aston-ishment, and everyone stared. "That won't do; that won't do at all. Look at your skin, man; it will register gray—and those lines—you can't use lines like that in the pictures. Roberts, go show him how to make up."

I thought of my first appearance in *Rags to Riches,* and felt almost as humiliated as I had then, while Roberts went with me to the dress-ing room and showed me how to coat my face and neck with a dull brick-brown paint, and to load my lashes heavily with black. The character lines I had drawn with such care would not do in the pic-tures, I learned, because they would show as lines. I must give the character effect by the muscles of my face.

Feeling very strange in this make-up, I went back the second time to the stage. The doctor, satisfied this time, gave me a few last directions and the pie, and I mounted to the top of the set.

"Remember, don't look at the camera, keep within range, throw yourself into the part and say anything that comes into your head," the director said. "All ready? Go to it."

The camera began to click; I clutched the pie, took a long breath, and tumbled through the trap door.

"Register surprise! Register surprise!" the director ordered in a low tense voice, while I struggled to get up without damaging the pie. I turned my head toward the clicking camera, and suddenly it seemed like a great eye watching me. I gazed into the round black lens, and it seemed to swell until it was yards across. I tried to pull my face into an expression of surprise, but the muscles were stiff and I could only stare fascinated at the lens. The clicking stopped.

"Too bad. You looked at the camera. Try it again," said the direc-tor, making a note of the number of feet of film spoiled. He was a very patient director; he stopped the camera and placed the pie on top of it for safety, while I fell through the trap door twice and twice played the scene through, using the pie tin. Then the pie was placed under my coat again, the camera began to click, and again I started the scene. But the clicking drew my attention to the lens in spite of myself. I managed to keep from looking directly at it, but I felt that my acting was stiff, and halfway through the scene the camera stopped again.

"Out of range," said the camera man carelessly, and lighted a ciga-rette. I had forgotten the circle of dots on the floor and crossed them.

I had eaten a large piece of the pie. There was a halt while another was brought, and the director, after an anxious look at the sun, used the interval in playing the scene through himself falling through the trap door, registering surprise and apprehension and panic at the proper points, and impressing upon me the way it was done. Then I tried it again.

All that afternoon I worked, black and blue from countless falls on the cement floor, perspiring in the intense heat, and eating no less than three large pies. They were cherry pies, and I had never cared much for them at any time.

When the light failed that evening the director, with a troubled frown, thoughtfully folded the working script and dismissed the camera man. Most of the actors in the other companies had gone; the wildreness of empty sets looked weird in the shadows. A boy appeared, caught the rats by their tails, and popped them back into their box.

"Well, that's all for today. We'll try it again tomorrow," the director said, not looking at me. "I guess you'll get the hang of it all right, after a while."

In my dressing room I scrubbed the paint from my face and neck with vicious rubs. I knew I had failed miserably and my self-esteem smarted at the thought. Even if I had succeeded, I said bitterly, what was the fun in a life like that? No excitement, no applause, just hard work all day and long empty evenings with nothing to do.

Only two considerations prevented me from canceling my contract and quitting at once—I was getting two hundred dollars a week, and I would not admit to myself that I—I, who had been a success with William Gillette and a star with Carno[1]—was a failure in the films. Nevertheless, I was in a black mood that night, and when after dinner the waiter, bending deferentially at my elbow, insinuated politely, "The cherry pie is very good, sir," he fell back aghast at the language I used.

Work at the studio began at eight next morning, and I arrived very tired and ill-tempered because of waking so early. We began immediately on the same scene, and after I had ruined some more film by unexpectedly landing on a rat when I fell through the trap door, we managed to get it done, to my relief. However, all that week, and the next, my troubles increased.

We played all the scenes which occurred in one set before we went on to the next set, so we were obliged to take the scenes at haphazard through the play, with no continuity or apparent connection. The interiors were all played on the stage, and most of the exteriors were taken "on location," that is, somewhere in the country. It was confusing, after being booted through a door, to be obliged to appear on the other side of it two days later, with the same expression, and complete the tumble begun fifteen miles away. It was still more confusing

[1] [Correctly spelled with a "K." Chaplin refers to the Fred Karno company.]

to play the scenes in reverse order, and I ruined three hundred feet of film by losing my hat at the end of a scene, when the succeeding one had already been played with my hat on.

At the end of the second week the comedy was all on the film and the director and I were being polite to each other with great effort. I was angry with everyone and everything, my nerves worn thin with the early hours and unaccustomed work, and he was worried because I had made him a week late in producing the film. The day the negative was done Mack Sennett arrived from New York, and I met him with a jauntiness which was a hollow mockery of my real feeling.

"Well, they tell me the film's done," he said heartily, shaking my hand. "Now you're going to see yourself as others see you for the first time. Is the darkroom ready? Let's go and see how you look on the screen."

The director led the way, and the three of us entered a tiny perfectly dark room. I could hear my heart beating while we waited, and talked nervously to cover the sound of it. Then there was a click, the shutter opened, and the picture sprang out on the screen. It was the negative, which is always shown before the real film is made, and on it black and white were reversed. It was several seconds before I realized that the black-faced man in white clothes, walking awkwardly before me, was myself. Then I stared in horror.

Funny? A blind man couldn't have laughed at it. I had ironed out entirely any trace of humor in the scenario. It was stiff, wooden, stupid. We sat there in silence, seeing the picture go on, seeing it become more awkward, more constrained, more absurd with every flicker. I felt as though the whole thing were a horrible nightmare of shame and embarrassment. The only bearable thing in the world was the darkness; I felt I could never come out into the light again, knowing I was the same man as the inane, ridiculous creature on the film. Halfway through the picture Mr. Sennett took pity on me and stopped the operator.

"Well, Chaplin, you didn't seem to get it that time," he said. "What's wrong, do you suppose?"

"I don't know," I said.

"Yes, it's plain we can't release this," the director put in moodily. "Two thousand feet of film spoiled."

"Oh, damn your film!" I burst out in a fury, and rising with a spring which upset my chair I slammed open the door and stalked out. "Well, here is where I quit the pictures," I thought.

Mr. Sennett and the director overtook me before I reached my dressing room and we talked it over. I felt that I would never make a moving-picture actor, but Mr. Sennett was more hopeful. "You're a crackerjack comedian," he said. "And you'll photograph well. All you need is to get camera-wise. We'll try you out in something else; I'll direct you, and you will get the hang of the work all right."

The director brought out a mass of scenarios which had been passed up to him by the scenario department and Mr. Sennett picked out one and ordered the working script of it made immediatley. Next day we set to work together on it. Mr. Sennett patient, good-humored, considerate, coaching me over and over in every gesture and expression; I with a hard, tense determination to make a success this time.

We worked another week on this second play, using every hour of good daylight. It was not entirely finished then, but enough was done to give an idea of its success, and again the negative was sent to the darkroom for review.

I went to see it with the sensations of dread and shrinking one feels at the sight of a dentist's chair, and my worst fears were justified. The film was worse than the first one—utterly stupid and humorless.

"Well, what are we going to do about it?" Mr. Sennett asked, when the flicker of the second film had ceased and we knew it a worse failure than the first. "Looks hopeless, doesn't it?"

"Yes," I said, with a sinking heart, for after all I had had a flicker of hope for success this time. We had both worked hard, and now we were tired and discouraged. I went alone to my dressing room, shut the door, and sat down to think it over.

The trouble with the films, I decided, was lack of spontaneity. I was stiff; I took all the surprise out of the scenes by anticipating the next motion. When I walked against a tree, I showed that I knew I would hit it, long before I did. I was so determined to be funny that every muscle in my body was stiff and serious with the strain. And then that confounded clicking of the camera and the effort it took to keep from looking at it—and the constant fear of spoiling a foot of film.

"So you're a failure," I said, looking at myself in the mirror. "You're a failure; no good; down and out. You can't make a cinema film. You're beaten by a click and an inch of celluloid. You *are* a rotter, no mistake!"

I was so furious at that that I smashed the mirror into bits with my fist. I walked up and down the dressing room, hating myself and the camera and the film and the whole detestable business. I thought of haughtily stalking out and telling Mr. Sennett I was through with the whole thing; I was going back to London, where I was appreciated. Then I knew he would be glad to let me go; he would say to himself that I was no good in the pictures, and I would always know it was true. My vanity ached at the thought. No matter how much success I made, no matter how loud the audience applauded, I would always say to myself, "Very well for you, but you know you failed in the cinemas."

With a furious gesture I grabbed my hat and went out to find Mr. Sennett. He was on the stage watching the work of another company. I walked up to him in a sort of cold rage and said, "See here, Mr. Sennett, I can succeed in this beastly work. I know I can. You let me have a chance to do things the way I want to and I'll show you."

"I don't know what I can do. You've had the best scenarios we've got, and we haven't hurried you," he said reasonably. "You know the rest of the companies get out two reels a week, and we've taken three weeks to do what we've done with you—about a reel and a half."

"Yes, but the conditions are all wrong," I hurried on. "Rehearsing over and over, and no chance to vary an inch, and then that clicking beginning just when I start to play. And I miss a cane. I have to have a cane to be funny."

It must have sounded childish enough. Mr. Sennett looked at me in surprise.

"You can have a cane, if that's what you want. But I don't know how you are going to make pictures without rehearsing and without a camera," he said.

"I want to make up my own scenarios as I go along. I just want to go out on the stage and be funny," I said. "And I want the camera to keep going all the time, so I can forget about it."

"Oh, see here, Chaplin, you can't do that. Do you know what film costs? Four cents a foot, a thousand feet of film. You'd waste thousands of dollars' worth of it in a season. You see that yourself. Great Scott, man, you can't take pictures that way!"

"You give me a chance at it, and I'll show you whether I can or not," I replied. "Let me try it, just for a day or so, just one scene. If the film's spoiled, I'll pay for it myself."

We argued it out for a long time. The notion seemed utterly crazy to Mr. Sennett, but after all I had made a real success in comedy, and his disappointment must have been great at my failure on the films. Finally he consented to let me try making pictures my way, on condition that I should pay the salary of the operator and the cost of the spoiled film.

That night I walked up and down the street for hours, planning the outlines of a scenario and the make-up I would wear. My cane, of course, and the loose baggy trousers which are always funny on the stage, I don't know why. I debated a long time about the shoes. My feet are small, and I thought perhaps they might seem funnier in tight shoes, under the baggy trousers. At last, however, I decided on the long, flat, floppy shoes, which would trip me up unexpectedly.

These details determined upon, I was returning to my hotel when suddenly I discovered I was hungry, and remembered that I had eaten no dinner. I dropped into a cafeteria for a cup of coffee, and there I saw a mustache. A little clipped mustache, worn by a very dignified solemn gentleman who was eating soup. He dipped his spoon into the bowl and the mustache quivered apprehensively. He raised the spoon and the mustache drew back in alarm. He put the soup to his lips and the mustache backed up against his nose and clung there.

It was the funniest thing I had ever seen. I choked my coffee, gasped, finally laughed outright. I must have a mustache like that!

Next day, dressed in the costume I had chosen, I glued the mustache to my lip before the dressing-room mirror, and shouted at the reflection. It was funny; it was uproariously funny! It waggled when I laughed, and I laughed again. I went out on the stage still laughing, and followed by a shout of mirth from every one who saw me. I tripped on my cane, fell over my shoes, got the cameraman to shouting with mirth. A crowd collected to watch me work, and I plunged into my first scene in high spirits.

I played the scene over and over, introducing funnier effects each time. I enjoyed it thoroughly, stopping every time I got out of the range of the camera to laugh again. The other actors, watching behind the camera, held their sides and howled, as my old audiences had done when I was with Carno. "This," I said to myself triumphantly. "This is going to be a success!"

When the camera finally stopped clicking all my old self-confidence and pride had come back to me. "Not so bad, what?" I said, triumphantly twirling my cane, and in sheer good spirits I pretended to fall against the camera, wringing a shout of terror from the operator. Then, modestly disclaiming the praises of the actors, though indeed I felt they were less than I deserved, I went whistling to my dressing-room.

"How soon do you want to see the film, Mr. Chaplin?" the operator asked, tapping at my door while I was changing into street clothes.

"Just as soon as you can have it, old top," I replied cheerfully. "Oh, by the way, how many feet did we use?"

"Little over two thousand," he called back, and I heard the sound of his retreating feet.

A little over two thousand! At four cents a foot! Eighty dollars! I felt as though a little cold breeze was blowing on my back. Nearly a month's salary with Carno wagered on the success of three hours' work! After all, I thought, I was not sure how the film would turn out; the beastly machine might not see the humor of my acting, good as it had been. I finished dressing in a hurry, and went out to find Mr. Sennett and show him the film in the darkroom.

I sat on the edge of my chair in the darkroom, waiting for the picture to flash on the screen, thinking of that eighty dollars, which alternately loomed large as a fortune and sank into insignificance. If the picture was good— But suppose it, too, was a failure! Then I would be stranded in California, thousands of miles from home, and where would I get the eighty dollars?

The shutter clicked open and the negative began to flicker on the screen. I saw myself, black-faced, with a little white mustache and enormous white shoes, walking in great dignity across the patch of light. I saw myself trip over my shoes. I saw the mustache quiver with alarm. I saw myself stop, look wise, twirl my cane knowingly, and hit myself on the nose. Then, suddenly in the stillness, I heard a loud chuckle from Mr. Sennett. The picture was good. It was very good.

"Well, Chaplin, you've done it! By George, you've certainly got the comedy! It's a corker!" Mr. Sennett said, clapping me heartily on the back as we came out of the darkroom. "You've wasted a lot of film, but hang the film! You're worth it! Go on and finish this up. I'd like to release it next week."

"We'll use the third scene," Mr. Sennett said to the camera operator. "How long will it run?"

"About two hundred feet," the operator replied.

"Well, keep it and throw away the rest. Think you can finish two good reels this week?" Mr. Sennett asked, turning to me.

"Watch me!" I responded airily, and my heart gave a great jump. They were paying me two hundred a week and were willing to throw away thousands of feet of film in addition to get my comedies. "There's a fortune in this business! A fortune!" I thought.

My ambition soared at that moment to dazzling heights. I saw myself retiring, after five or ten years in the business, with a fortune of ten thousand pounds—yes, even twenty thousand!

The comedy was finished that week; I worked every day, during every moment when the light was good, not stopping for luncheon or to rest. I enjoyed the work; the even click-click-click of the camera, running steadily, was a stimulant to me; my ideas came thick and fast. I sketched in my mind the outlines of a dozen comedies, to be played later. I remembered all the funny things I had seen or heard and built up rough scenarios around them. I woke in the night, chuckling at a new idea that occurred to me.

When my first comedy was released it was a great success. The producers demanded more, quickly. I was already working on *Caught in the Rain*. I followed it the next week with *Laughing Gas*. They all went big.

Every morning when I reached the stage in make-up the actors who were to play with me stood waiting to learn what their parts were to be. I myself did not always know, but when I had limbered up a bit by a jig or clog dance and the camera began to click, ideas came fast enough.

I told the other actors how to play their parts, played them myself to show how it should be done; played my own part enthusiastically, teased the cameraman, laughed and whistled and turned handsprings. The clicking camera took it all in; later, in the negative room, we chose and cut and threw away film, picking out the best scenes, re-arranging the reels, shaping up the final picture to be shown on the screens. I liked it all; I was never still a minute in the studio and never tired.

The only time I was quiet was while I was making up. Then I thought sometimes of my early days in England, of Covent Garden, and my mother and my year with William Gillette. "Life's a funny thing," I said to myself. Then I made up as a baker, ordered a wagon-load of bread dough and flour and went out and romped through it hilarious, shouting with laughter whenever I was out of range of the camera. The result was *Dough and Dynamite*, and it clinched what I then thought was my success in the movies.

At first when my pictures began to appear in the moving-picture houses I took great delight in walking among the crowds in front of the doors, idly twirling my cane and listening to the comments on my comedies. I liked to go inside, too, and hear the audiences laugh at the comical figure I cut on the screen. That was the way I got my first real ambition in motion-picture work. I still have it. I want to make people chuckle.

Audiences laugh in two ways. Upon the stage, in all the tense effort of being funny behind the footlights, I had never noticed that. But one night, packed with the crowd in a small, dark moving-picture house, watching the flickering screen, listening for the response of the people around me, I suddenly realized it.

I had wedged into a crowded house to see my latest film. It was a rough-and-tumble farce; the audience had been holding its sides and shrieking hysterically for five minutes. "Oh, ho!" I was saying to my-self. "You're getting 'em, old top, you're getting 'em!" Suddenly the laughter stopped.

I looked around dismayed. I could see a hundred faces, white in the dim light, intent on the picture—and not a smile on any of them. I looked anxiously at the screen. There was Charlie Chaplin in his make-up standing still. Standing still in a farce! I wondered how I had ever let a thing like that get past the negative. The house was still; I could hear the click of the unrolling film.

Then on the screen I saw myself turn slowly; saw my expression become grim and resolute; saw myself grip my cane firmly and stalk away. I was going after the husky laborer who had stolen my beer.

Then it came—a chuckle, a deep hearty "Ha! Ha! Ha!" It spread over the crowd like a wave; the house rocked with it.

"That's it! that's what I want, that's what I want!" I said. I got out quickly to think it over. I had to crowd past the knees of a dozen people to do it, and not one of them glared at me. They were still chuckling.

I walked back to my hotel with my cane tucked under my arm and my hands in my pockets. That was the thing—the chuckle! Any kind of laughter is good; any kind of laughter will get the big salaries. But a good, deep, hearty chuckle is the thing that warms a man's heart; it's the thing that makes him your friend; it's the thing that shows, when you get it, that you have a real hold on your audience. I have worked for it ever since.

After that I visited the picture houses night after night, watching for that chuckle, planning ways to get it. I was never recognized by strangers, and more than once some one asked me what I thought of Charlie Chaplin. I do not recall that I ever told the truth. In fact, I was not thinking much about Charlie Chaplin in those days; I was thinking of his work and his success and his growing bank account.

I had come into the business at the height of its first big success. Fortunes were being made overnight in it; producers could not turn out film fast enough to satisfy the clamoring public. The studios were like gambling houses in the wild fever of play. Money was nothing; it was thrown away by hundreds, by thousands. "Give us the film, give us the film! To hell with the expense!" was the cry. I heard of small tailors, of streetcar motormen, who had got into the game with a few hundred dollars and now were millionaires. In six months I was smiling at my early notion of making fifty thousand dollars.

Sidney, who was still in vaudeville, came to Los Angeles about that time, and I met him at the train with one of the company's big automobiles. The same old reliable Sidney with his sound business sense. He had figured out the trend of affairs and was already negotiating with the Essanay company for a good contract with them, going deliberately into the work I had blundered into by accident.

"There's a fortune in this if it's handled right, Charlie," he said.

"A fortune? If this holds out, if I can keep up my popularity, I'll have a cool half million before I quit, my lad! Keep your eye piped for your Uncle Charlie!" I said gaily.

WORKING METHOD

Development of the Comic Story and the Tramp Character
by CHARLIE CHAPLIN

Most of the little plays in which I have appeared in moving pictures I have written myself. I learn something new every day. All there is in moving-picture comedy is to study the fundamentals. After all, that's all there is in life, and it takes a lifetime to find them out. If I were to attempt to explain the method by which my share of success in moving pictures has been obtained, they would not apply for someone else to work out. My methods are my own, created and developed to reflect my personality, and what is best for me and my work. There may be technical rules in comedy, but I don't think you could standardize them. Comedy is the most serious study in the world.

There is no study in the art of acting that requires such an accurate and sympathetic knowledge of human nature as comedy work. To be successful in it, one must acquire the gift of studying men at their daily work.

When I write a new play for the screen, I lay out my plot first, then I put it aside, and I start out to find my characters in real life. First of all, of course, I search for the man I am going to represent myself. When I find that man, I follow him, watch him at his work, and his fun, at the table, and every other place I can see him. Often, I will study one man for a week before I am ready to go on with the play. Generally, the best situations in a play, the funniest, will either be an exaggeration of such action in real life that I have seen my counterpart pass through, but which was not at all funny in itself.

I have always tried to avoid burlesque, or at least not to depend upon it. I strive for naturalness in all my action. One of the best instances of how I put a play together and how I worked to develop it, is in the story of one of my plays called *The Tramp.*

From "How I Made My Success" by Charlie Chaplin, The Theatre *22 (September 1915): 121, 142.*

The inspiration for it came from an accidental meeting with a hobo in a street in San Francisco. He had the usual symptoms of his class, he was suffering a little from lack of food, and intensely from lack of drink. I made a cheerful proposition to him, offering him both, and asking him which he would have first.

"Why," he said, "if I get hungry enough, I can eat grass. But, what am I going to do for this thirst of mine? You know what water does to iron? Well, try to think what it will do for your insides."

We went into a barroom, he got the drink, and we sat right down then and there to have a bite of lunch. The food and drink warmed him and brought to the surface the irresponsible joy of life possessed by the nomad and the ne'er-do-well. He told me the story of his life. Of long jaunts through the beautiful country, of longer rides on convenient freights, of misfortunes which attend the unfortunate who are found stealing a ride on a "side-door pullman," and of the simplicity of the farmers who lived only a short distance from the city. It was a delight to hear him talk, to gather from it the revelations of his character, to watch his gestures, and his trick of facial expression. All these elements were carefully watched by me, and noted for future reference. He was rather surprised when we parted, at my profuse thanks. He has given me a good deal more than I had given him, but he didn't know it. He had only obtained a little food and drink and a chance talk from me. From him, I had a brand new idea for a picture.

The moment I left him, I sat down to develop my plot. The play was really written around a character from life. I imagined him on some of his wanderings through the country. I introduced the situation of a beautiful country girl befriending him. Remembering his contempt for rural people and things, I constructed an imaginary series of episodes dealing with his life on the farm. I invented the situation of his falling in love with the girl; my tramp friend did not suggest any romance in his hobo life. With the completion of the scenario came the real work.

It took three weeks' hard labor to complete that two-reel comedy. I worked with every individual actor. I explained to them the tramp's point of view, and I tried to make them respond as country people would to a tramp. At first the other actors could not grasp the idea. That was very natural, because the idea was mine, and I had to give it to others before they could make it live. We rehearsed over fifty times some of the small situations. A little thing like the twist of a foot on a ladder, or dropping a bag of meal on a man's head, took hours and hours of time. This was because I was striving for naturalness, and it meant intense concentration and hard work for all of us.

The Essanay management have made this problem much easier for me, however, thanks to an arrangement by which I have the use of a studio in Los Angeles set apart entirely for my own plays, and a little selected company of players, who work with me in all my releases. They have grown used to my methods, my effects, and purposes, so that the working out of a new play under these conditions is a pleasure.

They know that I find naturalness in the screen comedy by studying my characters and situations in real life, and they have adapted my plan.

Most of the fun in *Work*, one of my very latest releases, comes through the efforts of a painter's assistant to push a two-wheeled barrow loaded with materials. This idea came to me from a scene I witnessed, one that was not funny for the assistant, but very laughable for the bystanders. The man was trying to get up hill, and the weight of the barrow kept pulling him up in the air, and letting him down again, until finally he was carried in a half circle over his barrow wheel and the contents were spilled. I enlarged the idea, and the audiences shout with amusement.

What People Laugh At
by CHARLIE CHAPLIN

. . . Comedy moving pictures were an instant success because most of them showed policemen falling down coalholes, slipping into buckets of whitewash, falling off patrol wagons, and getting into all sorts of trouble. Here were men representing the dignity of the law, often very pompous themselves, being made ridiculous and undignified. The sight of their misfortunes at once struck the public funny bone twice as hard as if private citizens were going through like experience.

Even funnier than the man who has been made ridiculous, however, is the man who, having had something funny happen to him, refuses to admit that anything out of the way has happened, and attempts to maintain his dignity. Perhaps the best example is the intoxicated man who, though his tongue and walk give him away, attempts in a dignified manner to convince you that he is quite sober.

He is much funnier than the man who, wildly hilarious, is frankly drunk and doesn't care a whoop who knows it. Intoxicated characters on the stage are almost always "slightly tipsy" with an attempt at dignity, because theatrical managers have learned that this attempt at dignity is funny.

For that reason, all my pictures are built around the idea of getting me into trouble and so giving me the chance to be desperately serious in my attempt to appear as a normal little gentleman. That is why, no matter how desperate the predicament is, I am always very much in earnest about clutching my cane, straightening my derby hat, and fixing my tie, even though I have just landed on my head.

I am so sure of this point that I not only try to get myself into embarrassing situations, but I also incriminate the other characters in the picture. When I do this, I always aim for economy of means. By that I mean that when one incident can get two big, separate laughs, it is much better than two individual incidents. In *The Adventurer*, I accomplished this by first placing myself on a balcony, eating ice cream

From American Magazine *86 (November 1918):* 34, 134–37.

with a girl. On the floor directly underneath the balcony I put a stout, dignified, well-dressed woman at a table. Then, while eating the ice cream, I let a piece drop off my spoon, slip through my baggy trousers, and drop from the balcony onto this woman's neck.

The first laugh came at my embarrassment over my own predicament. The second, and the much greater one, came when the ice cream landed on the woman's neck and she shrieked and started to dance around. Only one incident had been used, but it had got two people into trouble, and had also got two big laughs.

Simple as this trick seems there were two real points of human nature involved in it. One was the delight the average person takes in seeing wealth and luxury in trouble. The other was the tendency of the human being to experience within himself the emotions he sees on the stage or screen.

One of the things most quickly learned in theatrical work is that people as a whole get satisfaction from seeing the rich get the worst of things. The reason for this, of course, lies in the fact that nine tenths of the people in the world are poor, and secretly resent the wealth of the other tenth.

If I had dropped the ice cream, for example, on a scrubwoman's neck, instead of getting laughs, sympathy would have been aroused for the woman. Also, because a scrubwoman has no dignity to lose, that point would not have been funny. Dropping ice cream down a rich woman's neck, however, is, in the minds of the audience, just giving the rich what they deserve.

By saying that human beings experience the same emotions as the people in the incidents they witness, I mean that—taking ice cream as an example—when the rich woman shivered the audience shivered with her. A thing that puts a person in an embarrassing predicament must always be perfectly familiar to an audience, or else the people will miss the point entirely. Knowing that ice cream is cold, the audience shivers. If something was used that the audience did not recognize at once, it would not be able to appreciate the point as well. On this same fact was based the throwing of custard pies in the early pictures. Everyone knew that custard pie is squashy, and so was able to appreciate how the actor felt when one landed on him.

Many persons have asked me where I got the idea for the type of the character I play. Well, all I can say is that it is a composite picture of many Englishmen I had seen in London during the years of my life in that city.

When the Keystone Film Company, with which I made my first pictures, asked me to leave Karno's *Night in an English Music Hall*, a pantomime in which I was playing, I was undecided what to do about the offer, principally because I did not know what kind of a comedy character I could play. Then, after a time, I thought of all the little Englishmen I had seen with small black mustaches, tight-fitting clothes, and bamboo canes, and I decided to model my make-up after these men.

Thinking of the cane was perhaps the best piece of luck I ever had. One reason is that the cane places me, in the minds of the audience, more quickly than anything else could. The other is that I have developed the cane until it has almost a comedy sense of its own. Often, I find it curling itself around someone's leg, or rapping someone on the shoulder and getting a laugh from the audience almost without my knowing that I was directing its action. . . .

Very often I hear a slight ripple at something I had not expected to be funny. At once I prick up my ears and ask myself why that particular thing got a laugh.

In a way, my going to see a movie is really the same as a merchant observing what people are wearing or buying or doing. Anyone who caters to the public has got to keep his knowledge of "what people like" fresh and up to date.

In the same way that I watch people inside a theater to see when they laugh, I watch them everywhere to get material which they can laugh at.

I was passing a firehouse one day, for example, and heard a fire alarm ring in. I watched the men sliding down the pole, climbing onto the engine, and rushing off to the fire. At once a train of comic possibilities occurred to me. I saw myself sleeping in bed, oblivious to the clanging of the fire bell. This point would have a universal appeal, because everyone likes to sleep. I saw myself sliding down the pole, playing tricks with the fire horses, rescuing the heroine, falling off the fire engine as it turned a corner, and many other points along the same lines. I stored these points away in my mind and some time later, when I made *The Fireman,* I used every one of them. Yet if I had not watched the firehouse that day the possibilities in the character of a fireman might never have occurred to me.

Another time, I went up and down a moving staircase in a department store. I got to thinking how this could be utilized for a picture, and I finally made it the basis of *The Floorwalker.* Watching a prize fight suggested *The Champion,* in which I, the small man, knocked out a big bruiser by having a horseshoe concealed in my glove. In another picture I used an employment office as the foundation of the picture. In other words, it has paid me to be always alive to the comic possibilities of the people and the things I see in everyday life.

I was seated in a restaurant once, for example, when I suddenly noticed that a man a few yards away kept bowing and smiling, apparently at me. Thinking he wished to be friendly, I bowed and smiled back at him. As I did this, however, he suddenly scowled at me. I thought I had been mistaken in his intentions. The next minute, however, he smiled again. I bowed; but once more he scowled. I could not imagine why he was smiling and scowling until, looking over my shoulder, I saw he had been flirting with a pretty girl. My mistake made me laugh, and yet it was a natural one on my part. So when the opportunity came a few months ago to utilize such a scene in *A Dog's Life*, I made use of the incident.

Another point about the human being that I use a great deal is the liking of the average person for contrast and surprise in his entertainment. It is a matter of simple knowledge, of course, that the human likes to see the struggle between the good and the bad, the rich and the poor, the successful and the unsuccessful. He likes to cry and he likes to laugh, all within the space of a very few moments. To the average person, contrast spells interest, and because it does I am constantly making use of it in my pictures.

If I am being chased by a policeman, I always make the policeman seem heavy and clumsy while, by crawling through his legs, I appear light and acrobatic. If I am being treated harshly, it is always a big man who is doing it; so that, by the contrast between big and little, I get the sympathy of the audience, and always I try to contrast my seriousness of manner with the ridiculousness of the incident.

It is my luck, of course, that I am short, and so am able to make these contrasts without much difficulty. Everyone knows that the little fellow in trouble always gets the sympathy of the mob. Knowing that it is part of human nature to sympathize with the "underdog," I always accentuate my helplessness by drawing my shoulders in, drooping my lip pathetically and looking frightened. It is all part of the art of pantomime, of course. But if I were three inches taller it would be much more difficult to get the sympathy of the audience. I should then look big enough to take care of myself. As it is, the audience, even while laughing at me, is inclined to sympathize with me. As someone once said, it feels like "mothering me."

However, one has got to be careful to make the contrast clear enough. At the close of *A Dog's Life*, for example, I am supposed to be a farmer. Accordingly, I thought it might be funny for me to stand in a field, take one seed at a time from my vest pocket, and plant it by digging a hole with my finger. So I told one of my assistants to pick out a farm where this scene could be taken.

Well, he picked out a nice farm; but I did not use it, for the simple reason that it was too small! It did not afford sufficient contrast for my absurd way of planting the seed. It might be slightly funny on a small farm, but done on a large one of about 600 acres, the scene gets a big laugh, simply because of the contrast between my method of planting and the size of the farm.

On almost a par with contrast, I would put surprise.

Surprise has always seemed interesting to me because it is somewhat like news. Whenever I read the newspaper, I am always being surprised at what has happened in the world since yesterday. If, however, before I pick up the newspaper I knew exactly what was going to be in it, I should not be surprised, and therefore not so interested.

I not only plan for surprise in the general incidents of a picture, but I also try to vary my individual actions so that they, too, will come as a surprise. I always try to do the unexpected in a novel way. If I think an audience expects me to walk along the street while in a picture, I will suddenly jump on a car. If I want to attract a man's attention, instead of tapping him on the shoulder with my hand or calling to him, I hook my cane around his arm and gently pull him to me.

Figuring out what the audience expects, and then doing something different, is great fun to me. In one of my pictures, *The Immigrant*, the opening scene showed me leaning far over the side of a ship. Only my back could be seen and from the convulsive shudders of my shoulders it looked as though I was seasick. If I had been, it would have been a terrible mistake to show it in the picture. What I was doing was deliberately misleading the audience. Because, when I straighted up, I pulled a fish on the end of a line into view, and the audience saw that, instead of being seasick, I had been leaning over the side to catch the fish. It came as a total surprise and got a roar of laughter.

There is such a thing, however, as being too funny. There are some plays and pictures at which the audience laughs so much and so heartily that it becomes exhausted and tired. To make an audience roar is the ambition of many actors, but I prefer to spread the laughs out. It is much better when there is a continual ripple of amusement, with one or two big "stomach laughs," than when an audience "explodes" every minute or two.

People often ask me if all my ideas work out, and if it is easy to make a funny picture. I sometimes wish they could follow the whole process of getting the idea, working out the characters, taking the film, editing and arranging it.

I am often appalled at the amount of film I have to make in getting a single picture. I have taken as much as 60,000 feet in order to get the 2,000 feet seen by the public. It would take about twenty hours to run off 60,000 feet on the screen! Yet that amount must be taken to present forty minutes of picture.

Sometimes, when I find that, though I have worked hard over an idea, it has not yet taken final shape in my head, and is therefore not ready to be filmed, I at once drop it and try something else. I do not believe in wasting too much time on something that will not work out. I do believe in concentrating all your energies upon the thing you are doing. But if you can't put it across, after having done your best, try something else for a time, and then come back to your original scheme if you still have faith in it. That is the way I have always worked.

In my work I don't trust anyone's sense of humor but my own. There have been times when the people around the studio have screamed at certain scenes while the picture was in the making, and yet I have discarded those scenes because they did not strike me as being funny enough. It isn't because I think I am so much smarter than those around me. It is simply because I am the one who gets all the blame or credit for the picture. I can't insert a title in a picture, for instance, and say:

"People, I don't blame you for not laughing. I didn't think this was funny myself, but the fellows around me told me it was and so I let it go."

Here is another point that makes it difficult for me to trust the judgment of those around me. My cameraman and other assistants are so used to me that they don't laugh very much at what I do in rehearsal. If I make a mistake, however, then they laugh. And I, not realizing perhaps that I have made a mistake, am likely to think the scene is funny. I didn't get onto this point until I asked some of them one day why they had laughed at a bit of business that I did not think was amusing. When they told me they had laughed because I had done something wrong, I saw how they might mislead me. So now I am glad they don't always laugh at my stuff.

One of the things I have to be most careful about is not to overdo a thing, or to stress too much any particular point. I could kill laughs more quickly by overdoing something than by any other method. If I made too much of my peculiar walk, if I were too rough in turning people upside down, if I went to excess in anything at all, it would be bad for the picture. Restraint is a great word, not only for actors but for everybody to remember. Restraint of tempers, appetites, desires, bad habits, and so on, is a mighty good thing to cultivate.

One of the reasons I hated the early comedies in which I played was because there couldn't be much "restraint" in hurling custard pies! One or two custard pies are funny, perhaps; but when nothing but custard pies is used to get laughs, the picture becomes monotonous. Perhaps I do not always succeed by my methods, but I would a thousand times rather get a laugh through something clever and original than through slapstick and horseplay.

Max Linder's and Elsie Codd's Views on the Working Method

by LOUIS DELLUC

MAX LINDER

"When you see a Chaplin film," says Linder, "it is easy to realize that there is a great deal of work in it. Nevertheless, however well informed you may be, it is impossible to get any idea of the continuous and highly intelligent effort of Charlie Chaplin in his work. He calls me his teacher, but, for my part, I have been lucky to get lessons at his school. There are many stupid stories about Chaplin: in the first place he is English, and not French or Spanish as has been said. It was I who first told him that in France he was called Charlot and his brother Sidney, Julot. They were greatly amused and went about calling each other those names all day and bursting into laughter. Charlie has been a performer from his earliest days, and he was quite a remarkable musician and composer.

"Chaplin has built his own theater at Los Angeles, where he makes his pictures himself, with the collaboration of his brother and a dozen assistants for the stage setting. He works for the camera with the minutest care. The theater, of course, is equipped with all the most modern improvements and apparatus, but the secret is not in the mechanical work. It is in the method. Charlie, like the true humorist he is, has studied laughter with care, and knows how to provoke it with the rarest precision. He leaves nothing to the chance of improvization. He goes over and over scenes until he is satisfied. He 'shoots' every single rehearsal and has them thrown on the screen several times, so that he may find just the flaw which spoils the effect he is striving after. He keeps on starting again until he is content, and he is far harder to please than his most harshly critical spectator.

From Charlie Chaplin *by Louis Delluc, translated by Hamish Miles* (*London: The Bodley Head, 1922*), *pp. 33–50.*

"Seeing Charlie at work, I realize more clearly than ever how little count should be taken of the amount of negative that is used in making a picture. Over here we count up the number of feet as if it had some connection with the finished article. But in reality the only thing that has any connection with the quality of the film is the care taken in producing the picture. To give exact figures on this point, Chaplin spent two months in making a picture of 1,800 feet; he used for that more than 36,000 feet of negative; every scene was 'shot' twenty times; and with trials and alterations and finishing touches, that meant about fifty rehearsals.

"It has doubtless been noticed that Charlie never speaks and that his films have very few captions. I need not expound his qualities as an actor, for it is enough to see a film to admire and like them. What is less appreciated is the happy inspiration of his *mise-en-scène,* which he carries out himself. As a producer, he is deliberate and richly gifted; he knows how to construct and work up his film so as to bring out his qualities into sharp relief and to emphasize them by all the external action. His powers of observation have been mentioned, and to express the variety of feelings it is not enough to be merely an actor. There must also be a *mise-en-scène* which will draw out and bring into play the gifts of the interpreter. And Charlie Chaplin knows to a wonderful nicety how to make use of himself, and of his partners, so as to touch just the required note.

"The desired expression comes precisely at the instant when it is needed for the effect. From first to last, spectators of every race and of every type of mind follow the evolution of his thought, and in the very finest touches of his wit. Look at *One A.M.* Has not Charlie won his wager that he would keep the crowd laughing at the screen for a full half-hour? For that it is essential that he can be easily followed in his chosen theme, and, without wishing to take away any credit from his valuable fellow players, it can truly be said that Charlie owes the lion's share of his success to himself as actor and as manager. From the day when he became his own manager, his films have been on a higher plane of achievement.

"Chaplin works with a persevering obstinacy that must be unrivalled. This man in his thirties has already grey hairs about his temples.

"In spite of his fame and his millions, he remains very unaffected, very goodhearted, and a very good friend. With the other luminaries of his profession he is on the best of terms, and is a particularly close friend of Douglas Fairbanks, himself also a charming fellow, and with Mary Pickford, a delightful companion. Chaplin is very gay, one might almost say boyishly so. He is always wide awake, and, wearing his heart on his sleeve, is extremely charitable, always ready to lend a helping hand to all the good works that ask his help.

"He allows hardly anyone to enter his theater when work is going on. Jealous of his achievement, he is annoyed and rather distressed to find that, instead of seeking to create for themselves, other comic actors—American for the most part—only try to make an inferior imitation of himself, and use the slimmest of tricks to get at the secrets of his work. He was good enough to admit me to see him at work, and I can honestly say that he has no secrets. He is methodical to an unheard-of degree, and he has gifts that no imitation can touch. He has no dodges, no private inventions, but he is very intelligent, very systematic, very conscientious. One can understand why he is anxious to remain undisturbed while pictures are being made and to avoid the tiresome imitator. He was very displeased to hear that certain plagiarists in Paris were making use of his name, and had the intention of prosecuting them, but I advised him not to pay them such a tribute. He intends to come to France when he is able, for he cherishes a great affection for France, and during the war lent his aid, in the most disinterested fashion, to Allied propaganda and later to American patriotic purposes. In this latter connection he made a great tour on behalf of the Liberty Loan, and, as was to be expected from his popularity in the States, with the most impressive results. When this was concluded he returned to studio work, and we can confidently await his latest films as worthy successors to the unforgettable Mutual series.

"I have noticed certain writers speaking rather scornfully of Charlie, as if the power of making one's fellows laugh by perfectly proper means and real psychological study deserved contempt. As for those who don't find him funny, I don't know if they have seen him, and in any case they certainly form only a minute proportion among his spectators. Those who do not care for him do not know him properly, or confound him with some of his weakly [sic] imitators. Can there really be any doubt of the pains that must be taken to make men laugh, and is it not particularly unfair to throw scorn on us because we seek to give a moment's distraction to the vast public of the cinema? For laughter is one of man's greatest possessions, indispensable to moral health and balance.

"And what nonsense to say that Charlie and others are laughter makers only because they cut capers. It is impossible to make laughter merely with capers; they must be cut comically. Here and there a laugh can be got in the theater or music hall by an instinctive natural effect, and a gift for that may suffice to make a successful actor. But in the cinema that is virtually impossible, for there it is only possible to show off such natural gifts by care in preparation and intelligence of technique which are not sufficiently appreciated. Instinct may discover points, but they have to be translated into this special language of the screen, the effects reduced to their elements, their range accurately estimated, their exposition set out by careful stages. The imitators of Chaplin succeed to perfection in executing the same tricks as he does, but why do they not provoke the same laughter? Let the scoffers try a few of these 'capers' before the camera lens. They will soon see if one is as good as another. And between the lines of such writers one can read a reproach that the film comedians make millions of money. But do they believe that the people who offer them these sums are making a bad bargain? Whom are the actors cheating? They make this money by raising laughter if they can. A man like Chaplin makes the half of mankind laugh several times a year. Is not that worth a few millions?

"But the public has already made answer enough to the critics. The public is sovereign judge, and I think it is only the public which has the quality to build up these great film reputations. Charlie's reputation is well enough established to need no justification. It deserves only to be studied and commented upon, for is it not the most convincing proof of the value in film production of supporting extraordinary talent with order and system and hard work?

"Charlie Chaplin, producer and actor, is in my opinion a perfect model for those who, if they want to accomplish anything on the cinema, will have to strive to study and understand him thoroughly. Imitation is merely a proof of inferiority and impotence. Chaplin has a special get-up; he is famous by his own physique and gait; he is a *genre* of his own. Take all that from him if you will; it is only a pointless theft. But to trace the reasons for his success and so to work out the formulas and the numeroous guiding lines—that is to learn the business in the best school. I shall be pardoned for speaking of Chaplin with warmth. Before knowing him I was only his warmest admirer. Today I am his friend."

ELSIE CODD

Thus Max Linder. And we may add to his pages a few which appeared in *Le Ciné pour Tous* a few months later. They are by Miss Elsie Codd, Charlie Chaplin's secretary, who is a kind of purveyor of the truth about the great little man. In constant and close touch with the comedian, she knows what kind of man he is and has observed better than anyone the exact details of his workmanship. She writes as follows:

" 'Dear Charlie,
'Why don't you give us more films?'

"That is the gist of a large number of the letters which Charlie Chaplin opens every morning. During the last couple of years he has produced his comedies at the rate of two in twelve months, and his admirers seem to think that something ought to be done about it.

"When Charlie Chaplin started on his astonishing career his comic films were made with the speed and regularity that comes of working to a timetable. But as he gradually became his own master, and made himself his own author and manager and his own chief interpreter to boot, he changed all that. He knows very clearly that there is nothing more difficult than the art of making really comical films, and the 1,800 feet of a Chaplin comedy are the harvest of several months of painstaking labor, and of patient and conscientious study, imposed by the innate artistic sense of this comic genius who finds it so hard to satisfy himself.

"One curious thing about Chaplin is that his hardest work is not his work in front of the camera. It has already been said that he 'writes' his own scenarios, the groundwork ideas for the comic scenes, but this should not be taken literally, because he never works with the help of his manuscript. Genius has its own rules, and Chaplin is generally regarded as a manager of a most peculiar kind, his method being to set at naught all the methods usually taken for granted.

"The first inspiration, the keynote for a new film, may often come from some laughable incident which happened in his presence and round which he will build up little by little a whole scenario. Take *The Floorwalker* for example. This was inspired by the spectacle of an enormous gentleman performing an involuntary fall on a moving stairway at a New York station. On the other hand, as in several of his latest pictures, Charlie's imagination may turn over some particular theme and make that the chief element in his next remedy for the pessimism of our days.

"And certainly if anyone imagines that making a comic film is just a great joke, I should like him to watch Chaplin, day by day, from the time when the scenario enters its period of mental incubation.

"Before the great idea comes there is always a long succession of bad-tempered days and troubled nights. His more circumspect friends keep a respectful distance. But, for the sake of more complete isolation, Charlie will frequently go off for some peaceful fishing to Catalina Island for a few days.

"Once his decision is taken, he comes back to his studio, gets his friends together and tells them of his intentions. He invites their own ideas on the subject, some of which he may use as a sort of mental punch-ball, but most of which are at once turned down. But once sure that the idea of the film is approved by his intimates, after going through an elaboration of perhaps a fortnight or perhaps a couple of months, his great concern is now to get it realized.

"And then the technical department begins to hustle. Orders flow in from the management, and every day the carpenters and engineers are working feverishly at the erection of a palace or a public house, a village, or a poor street or a smart one, as the case requires. Charlie may have given months to pondering the theme, but once he has fixed on it, no delay is tolerated. Lately we saw this well. The requirements of the moment called for the construction of a very complicated street scene, and Charlie would turn up every morning without fail, feverishly questioning everyone to find out why the whole thing was not yet finished. His attitude is quite pathetic; he seems almost broken-hearted, and gives vent to wails: 'Here am I, all ready to begin—and here I am, held up by some stupid business or other.'

"Now let us glance at Charlie at the scene of action, and observe a day's work.

"At nine o'clock sharp everything and everybody is ready for the fray. The usual members of the company are all dressed and made up as requirements demand, and each one has to be personally inspected by Chaplin himself. He reserves the right to add or cut out as he thinks fit. In some cases a certain arrangement of the characters may be necessary, and then the manager responsible for casting the characters will have to make his plans a day or two beforehand. Sometimes at nine o'clock, and sometimes a little later, Chaplin springs from his automobile, bolts into his own rooms, and shortly reappears in all the glory of the get-up which he has made supreme on the screen. Then he gathers his collaborators, gives them some account of all that they are going to do, and describes in detail the scene that is about to be played.

"Once things have begun, Charlie's transformation is complete. All the preoccupation he may have been under disappears, and to all about him he is like a happy child enjoying some astonishing game of pretending.

"And this frame of mind gets more pronounced. No one could have a group of more loyal and friendly comrades than his collaborators. I remember an old lady—only a 'super'—telling me of the pleasure she and her companions had found in working in company with Mr. Chaplin. 'He is so kind and patient, and above all he's so *different* somehow.' I can well believe it, for on more than one hot California day I have been able to watch Charlie Chaplin at work, and I have been amazed at his unflagging spirits. He seemed to make everyone forget how oppressively hot it was and how tired they all really were.

"Once he has made clear in full detail the subject which is being worked upon, Chaplin makes the actors rehearse their parts one by one, having previously tried the business himself. Without exaggeration I think I can say that he has played every character in every one of his comedies. The chatterbox of a woman prattling without pity or reserve, the policeman directing traffic, the ruffian whom one is always waiting to see come out of the shadow of a door—for all the roles he first gives the actor his hints, lightly sketched but certain in its details. Then the actor of the part plays it himself, while Charlie accompanies his miming with a continuous commentary of encouragement or criticism or kindly suggestions. 'Just ever so little more vigor in that fling of the arm, Tom. . . . Yes, that's it. You've got it.'

"And then, speaking to the player of a villain's part: 'I don't want any of the conventional business of the usual cinema traitor. Just get yourself used to the idea that you're a rascal who isn't an out-and-out bad one, but simply hasn't got any moral sense. Don't put on a savage look. And above all, don't *act!*'

" 'Don't *act!*' How often have I heard Chaplin end up with that recommendation! Surprising as it may seem to an actor, it has meant half of Chaplin's success in the art of making comic pictures. Sincerity gives the power of conviction, and from that comes the fact that some things which we couldn't accept from anyone else we take as perfectly natural from Charlie Chaplin.

"When the rehearsals are once finished, Chaplin devotes all his attention to the camera. He puts his eye to the viewfinder and decides from what angle the secene should be taken. Then the two operators get ready: they go on turning until the order is given to stop.

"A Chaplin film when shown is perhaps 1,800 or 2,400 feet in length. To make this finished article, some 18,000 or 30,000 feet of negative are used, thanks to the methods adopted by Chaplin. The fact is that there is no producer more hard to please or more painstaking than he. I have seen him 'shoot' one single scene over and over again, half a dozen times, so as to reach the highest possible pitch of perfection.

"Sometimes he is struck with a sudden new idea when the cameras have finished recording a scene. 'Suppose we make him wriggle out and get away while the policeman's talking with the other fellow,' he suggests to the bystanders. 'That should make them laugh.' And in this way the scene is corrected or lengthened, until Chaplin has got clear all that it is possible to extract from this new business. Quite often after a day of five or six hours' work he has 'shot' the spool length of a whole comedy. But as a matter of fact he has merely recorded a certain number of variations on a single theme, which, in their place in the final film, will take up only two or three minutes on the screen.

"The first step in the procedure of elimination comes the morning after the pictures are taken. Before beginning the day's regular work, Chaplin goes to the projection room, and everything that was taken the day before is thrown on the screen before him. He can then take note that the expression of his face was better on reel 39 than on number 37, but that the action towards the end of 37 was livelier than in the corresponding part of 39. And that means that in the final version the end of number 37 will be joined up with the beginning of 39, and that perhaps some detail from number 38 will save this last from total rejection.

"Chaplin himself carries out the building-up process of his films, and the editing of the few captions necessary to a full understanding of the story. He is very economical of captions, for he rightly believes that the public pays to see a film and not to read long explanations of it. The final title of the picture is usually his chief concern. In fact the title that you see on the screen is often the result of a sleepless night or of great mental concentration, shortly before the final version of the picture is sent for distribution.

"It is one of Chaplin's customs to have the film shown in public at one of the Los Angeles picture theaters, without any previous advertisement. This method, which is called 'trying it on the dog,' enables him to gauge its effect on an unexpectant audience, and to find in what direction the whole may be improved before its delivery to the distributor. Sometimes there is a detail in a scene which misses fire. Charlie notes that, and if possible will improve it with a caption which helps to make it understood. These performances are of great interest, not only as giving the chance of an astonishing insight into the psychology of the cinema public, but also because they show how fully Chaplin understands this public.

"I remember how disappointed he was once about some little scene. 'I didn't hear the kids laugh,' he said, and we knew that, in his judgement at any rate, this particular point had been a failure. Chaplin realizes that his world-wide success is in great measure based on the affection of millions of children, and he finds in their spontaneous delight the ultimate proof of success.

"For, to end with his own words, Charlie Chaplin declares: 'It is not we personally who are great. It's only our greatness in our relation with others that *counts.*'"

A Rejection of the Talkies
by CHARLIE CHAPLIN

Because the silent or nondialogue picture has been temporarily pushed aside in the hysteria attending the introduction of speech by no means indicates that it is extinct or that the motion picture screen has seen the last of it.[1] *City Lights* is evidence of this. In New York it is presented at the George M. Cohan Theater beginning Feb. 6. It is a nondialogue but synchronized film.

Why did I continue to make nondialogue films? The silent picture, first of all, is a universal means of expression. Talking pictures necessarily have a limited field, they are held down to the particular tongue of particular races. I am confident that the future will see a return of interest in nontalking productions because there is a constant demand for a medium that is universal in its utility. It is axiomatic that true drama must be universal in its appeal—the word elemental might be better—and I believe the medium of presentation should also be a universal rather than a restricted one.

Understand, I consider the talking picture a valuable addition to the dramatic art regardless of its limitations, but I regard it only as an addition, not as a substitute. Certainly it could not be a substitute for the motion picture that has advanced as a pantomimic art form so notably during its brief twenty years of storytelling. After all, pantomime has always been the universal means of communication. It existed as the universal tool long before language was born. Pantomime serves well where languages are in the conflict of a common ignorance. Primitive folk used the sign language before they were able to form an intelligible word.

From "Pantomime and Comedy" by Charlie Chaplin, The New York Times, January 25, 1931, sec. 8, p. 6. © 1931 by The New York Times Company. Reprinted by permission of the publisher.

[1] [If one compares Richard Meryman's interview with Chaplin (*Life* 62 [10 March 1967]: 80–94), it becomes evident that the comedian's views have changed very little since his formative days as an actor-director in the movies.]

At what point in the world's history pantomime first made its appearance is speculative. Undoubtedly it greatly antedates the first records of its part in Greek culture. It reached a highly definite development in Rome and was a distinct factor in the medieval mystery plays. Ancient Egypt was adept in its use, and in the sacrificial rites of Druidism and in the war dances of the aborigines of all lands it had a fixed place.

Pantomime lies at the base of any form of drama. In the silent form of the photoplay it is the keynote. In the vocal form it must always be an essential, because nonvisual drama leaves altogether too much to the imagination. If there is any doubt of this, an example is the radio play.

Action is more generally understood than words. The lift of an eyebrow, however faint, may convey more than a hundred words. Like the Chinese symbolism, it will mean different things, according to its scenic connotation. Listen to a description of some unfamiliar object —an African warthog, for example—then describe it; observe a picture of the animal and then note the variety of astonishment.

We hear a great deal about children not going to the movies any more, and it is undoubtedly true that hundreds of thousands of prospective film patrons, of future film-goers, young tots who formerly thrilled to the silent screen, do not attend any more because they are unable to follow the dialogue of talking pictures readily. On the other hand, they do follow action unerringly. This is because the eye is better trained than the ear. There is nothing in *City Lights* that a child won't follow easily and understand.

I am a comedian and I know that pantomime is more important in comedy than it is in pure drama. It may be even more effective in farce than in straight comedy. These two differ in that the former implies the attainment of humor without logical action—in fact, rather the reverse; and the latter achieves this attainment as the outcome of sheer legitimate motivation. Silent comedy is more satisfactory entertainment for the masses than talking comedy, because most comedy depends on swiftness of action, and an event can happen and be laughed at before it can be told in words. Of course, pantomime is invaluable in drama, too, because it serves to effect the gradual transition from farce to pathos or from comedy to tragedy much more smoothly and with less effort than speech can ever do.

I base this statement on recent observations; the sudden arrival of dialogue in motion pictures is causing many of our actors to forget the elementals of the art of acting. Pantomime, I have always believed and still believe, is the prime qualification of a successful screen player.

A truly capable actor must possess a thorough grounding in pantomime. Consider the Irvings, Coquelins, Bernhardts, Duses, Mansfields, and Booths, and you will find at the root of their art pantomime.

My screen character remains speechless from choice. *City Lights* is synchronized and certain sound effects are part of the comedy, but it is a nondialogue picture because I preferred that it be that, for the reasons I have given.

ESSAYS

The Art of Charles Chaplin
by MINNIE MADDERN FISKE

It will surprise numbers of well-meaning Americans to learn that a constantly increasing body of cultured, artistic people are beginning to regard the young English buffoon, Charles Chaplin, as an extraordinary artist, as well as a comic genius. To these Americans one may dare only to whisper that it is dangerous to condemn a great national figure thoughtlessly. First, let us realize that at the age of twenty-six Charles Chaplin (a boy with a serious, wistful face) has made the whole world laugh. This proves that his work possesses a quality more vital than mere clowning. Doubtless, before he came upon the scene there were many "comedians" who expressed themselves in grotesque antics and grimaces, but where among them was there one who at twenty-six made his name a part of the common language of almost every country, and whose little, baggy-trousered figure became universally familiar? To the writer Charles Chaplin appears as a great comic artist, possessing inspirational powers and a technique as unfaltering as Rejane's. If it be treason to Art to say this, then let those exalted persons who allow culture to be defined only upon their own terms make the most of it.

Apart from the qualified critics, many thoughtful persons are beginning to analyze the Chaplin performances with a serious desire to discover his secret for making irresistible entertainment out of more or less worthless material. They seek the elusive quality that leavens the lump of the usually pointless burlesques in which he takes part. The critic knows his secret. It is the old, familiar secret of inexhaustible imagination, governed by the unfailing precision of a perfect technique.

Chaplin is vulgar. At the present stage of his career he is frankly a buffoon, and buffoonery is and always has been tinctured with the vulgar. Broad comedy all the way through history has never been able to keep entirely free from vulgarity. There is vulgarity in the come-

From Harper's Weekly *62* (*May 6, 1916*): *494.*

dies of Aristophanes, and in those of Plautus and Terence and the Elizabethans, not excluding Shakespeare. Rabelais is vulgar, Fielding and Smollett and Swift are vulgar. Among the great comics there is vulgarity without end. Vulgarity and distinguished art can exist together. When a great buffoon like Chaplin is engaged in making people laugh at the broad and obvious facts of life, he is continually so near the line that separates good taste from bad taste that it is too much to expect him never to stray for a moment on the wrong side of the line. If, in the name of so-called refinement, we are going to obliterate Chaplin and set him down as not worth considering, we must wipe all buffoonery off the slate and lay down the absolute rule that it is not a legitimate part of public entertainment.

Further, we must remember that the medium of Charles Chaplin's expression is entirely new. He has had only two years to develop his particular phase of the moving picture art. We all know it to be still in its infancy. The serious side of this newest medium of expression has received more attention than the comic side. Why is it not probable that the comic side may develop to a point where Chaplin's art will have opportunity to express itself in really brilliant and significant burlesque?

Anyone who has seen the primitive and meaningless comic scenes in which Chaplin began his career will see the difficulties under which his art was at first forced to express itself. Undoubtedly he will fare better in the future. It is said that his newest travesty, now current, shows that with a really intelligent scenario to aid him he can be supremely comic and at the same time free from vulagrity. Those of us who believe that Charles Chaplin is essentially a great comic artist look forward to fine achievements. We think that we know, perhaps better than he knows himself, what he is capable of accomplishing, and we are confident that he will attain the artistic stature to which it seems he is entitled.

It was a very humble entrance—the entrance of Charles Chaplin into the realm of comic art. Anyone could see him for a few pennies. It is said he came from a life of sadness. And at twenty-six he has made the world laugh. Quite a beautiful thing to do!

Is the Charlie Chaplin Vogue Passing?
by HARCOURT FARMER

Is Chaplin a great artist in his peculiar line, or is he merely a phenomenally successful comedian? Much water has flowed under the bridges since the earliest Keystone releases, featuring the then unknown funmaker, burst upon a delighted public; and the rapid rise into amazing prominence of the grotesque little man with big feet had about it all the earmarks of wonder. From 1913 to 1919 is but a space of years to the ordinary man. To Chaplin it meant literally fame and fortune. It meant emerging from a mediocre obscurity to the full flame of universal notoriety. It meant the Chaplin Vogue.

A couple of years ago it would have been deemed treasonable to cast the smallest of critical stones at Chaplin. He was the biggest thing in laughs in the whole of America. Undeniably, he was IT. The children in their millions acclaimed him, and if you've got them for your public, you're safe. With a practical astuteness which is characteristic, Chaplin recognized this; he played for and at the kiddies. And the result went into round figures. . . .

But today is not a couple of years ago—and a review of Chaplin's last release, *Sunnyside,* fills the analytical mind with grim foreboding. It wasn't a success, to put it bluntly. And, honestly, when you consider all the Chaplin films in the order of their manufacture, can you truthfully call them great art? Even if you allow that *A Dog's Life* was funny—which many people deny—and even if you affirm that *Shoulder Arms* was not an uncouth reflection on army life but a clever satire, you must admit that these two films were, in essence, but a rehash of the earlier *Carmen,* just as *Carmen* was a recooking of *Behind the Screen,* and so on and so on.

In other words, I contend that the extraordinary Chaplin vogue is based upon the simple law of repetition—that each film contains precisely the same elements—that the appeal of every Chaplin picture is to the lowest human instincts—and that, in the natural course of

From Theatre Magazine 30 (October 1919): 249.

events, the Chaplin vogue in five years will be a thing of remote antiquity.

This may seem to many, a statement of the wildest. It isn't. It's a perfectly fair and logical conclusion, reached after years devoted to studying the Chaplin phenomenon. I don't mean that it has taken me years to come to these conclusions; that would be underrating my own intelligence; but I do mean that, in ample justice to Mr. Chaplin, I have deliberately withheld the writing of this article during a period long enough for Mr. Chaplin to prove the stuff he's made of. And, to my thinking, his last six pictures not only prove my case—they shout it.

And now, having cleared the deck with apologetics, let's to the hamstringing process. Every Chaplin picture, without exception, is constructed upon the psychological principle that pain is diverting—that you'll laugh at the concept of someone else suffering injury. And you *do*. When one of the bewhiskered artistes in a Chaplin exhibition picks up a pitchfork and delicately impales another member of the cast through the seat of his trousers—the packed mass in front of the screen chortles and screams and shrieks—and the exchange manager wires the returns to the head office. Upon this basis the whole Chaplin claim to fame rests. It is the undying principle behind all burlesque; it is the oldest form of comedy and it traces its way through civilization from the Greek era to the day of Harold Lloyd. Historically speaking, slapstick is as old as tragedy.

But slapstick in the hands of a clever, brainy comedian is endurable; handled by a man who is uninventive, unoriginal, frankly unamusing, it becomes unspeakably tedious. The Chaplin era has produced a dozen imitators, some of them horribly boresome, some of them openly objectionable, a few of them decidedly clever. And they are clever simply because they don't insult their public by offering them the same old situations, the same old bits of "business," the same old contortions. Now, if I assert that Chaplin hasn't progressed artistically since his first successes, I consider I'm putting it kindly.

The most case-hardened Chaplin admirer can hardly deny that the appeal contained in the Chaplin films is an extremely unintellectual one—that it's an appeal, as I said above, to the lowest human instincts. Now this may not matter in the least to Mr. Chaplin or to his multitude of managers; it may not concern the vast public a jot, but to those serious-minded people who see something in the movies besides slapstick, this will immediately suggest itself. That the indubitable artistic and mechanical improvements of the motion picture has been in spite of the Chaplin school of slapstick film, and not because of it. I'm not one of the highbrow cranks; and I'm normal enough to admit the need of plenty of comedy and to want it myself. But I want that comedy to be good, and when I say that, I'm the mouthpiece of thousands of other men who feel just the same way about it.

And now I want to answer the question I asked at the top of this article: Is Chaplin a great artist or—isn't he? Well, what's the little thing that makes one actor an Edwin Booth and another actor a nonentity? What's the difference between a John Barrymore and an unknown ham? The answer is *brains*. Barrymore mixes his colors with brains, consequently he's a great comedian. Chaplin, happening by the drift of circumstance to make a lucky strike in a low-comedy characterization, has repeated that particular role in every public appearance. And that's one reason why he isn't a great artist.

I can't imagine Mr. Barrymore "getting a laugh" by mishandling a custard pie, or by certain indelicacies with his trousers, nor can I imagine Mr. Chaplin giving us an original comedy conception. I don't hold any brief for either of them; but I know whose films will be preserved in years to come. And I strenuously object to incompetent persons styling Charles Chaplin a great artist, when he's nothing of the sort. Let us be unsentimental and reasonable. The funny walk, the acute gestures, the petite mustache, the grotesque shoes, the sporadic vulgarities—they've all given us a deal of unaffected pleasure in the past; they were quite all right in the days when people went into a movie to kill time—but can't we look for something better and funnier in the future?

Everybody's Language
by WINSTON CHURCHILL

Every cinema-goer is familiar with the Chaplin tramps, but I wonder how many of them have reflected how characteristically American are these homeless wanderers. In the dwindling ranks of the English tramps one finds all sorts of people—from the varsity graduate whose career has ended in ruin and disgrace, to the half-imbecile illiterate who has been unemployable since boyhood. But they all have one thing in common—they belong to the great army of the defeated. They still maintain the pretense of looking for work—but they do not expect to find it. They are spiritless and hopeless.

The American hobo of twenty-five years ago was of an entirely different type. Often he was not so much an outcast from society as a rebel against it. He could not settle down, either in a home or a job. He hated the routine of regular employment and loved the changes and chances of the road. Behind his wanderings was something of the old adventurous urge that sent the covered wagons lumbering across the prairie towards the sunset.

There were also upon the highways of America, in the old days of prosperity, many men who were not tramps at all in the ordinary sense of the term. They were traveling craftsmen, who would work in one place for a few weeks or months, and then move on to look for another job elsewhere. Even today, when work is no longer easy to secure, the American wanderer still refuses to acknowledge defeat.

That indomitable spirit is an integral part of the make-up of the screen Charlie Chaplin. His portrayal of the underdog is definitely American rather than British. The English workingman has courage in plenty, but those whom prolonged unemployment has forced on the road are nowadays usually broken and despairing. The Chaplin tramp has a quality of defiance and disdain.

But the American scene as a whole has influenced Chaplin—its variety, its color, its animation, its strange and spectacular contrasts. And

Excerpted from Collier's *96 (October 26, 1935): 24, 37–38.*

the States did more than this for the little English actor; they provided the opportunity for which, without knowing it, he had been waiting. They introduced him to the ideal medium for his genius, the motion picture. . . .

It is Mr. Chaplin's dream to play tragic roles as well as comic ones. The man whose glorious fooling made *Shoulder Arms* a favorite with war-weary veterans of the trenches wants to reinterpret Napoleon to the world. There are other characters, as far removed from those in which he won preeminence, which he desires to portray.

Those who smile at these ambitions have not appreciated Chaplin's genius at its true worth. No mere clown, however brilliant, could ever have captured so completely the affections of the great public. He owes his unrivaled position as a star to the fact that he is a great actor, who can tug at our heartstrings as surely as he compels our laughter. There are moments, in some of his films, of an almost unbearable poignancy.

It is a great achievement, and one possible only to a consummate actor, to command at once tears and laughter. But it is the laughter which predominates, and Mr. Chaplin is perfectly right in desiring an opportunity of playing straight tragedy. Until he does so, his pathos will be regarded as merely a by-product of his toothbrush mustache and the ludicrous Chaplin walk.

I believe that, had it not been for the coming of the talkies, we would already have seen this great star in a serious role. He is the one figure of the old silent screen to whom the triumph of the spoken word has meant neither speech nor extinction. He relies, as of old, upon a pantomime that is more expressive than talk. But while the silence of Charlie Chaplin has lost none of its former magic, would Mr. Charles Chaplin, in a role of a kind completely unfamiliar to his audiences, and of which they would almost certainly be highly critical, be able to "get away with it"? . . .

It is the supreme achievement of Mr. Chaplin that he has revived in modern times one of the great arts of the ancient world—an art the secret of which was as completely and, apparently, as irrevocably lost as that of those glowing colors, fresh and vivid today as when they were first applied, which were the glory of the van Eycks.

The golden age of pantomime was under the early Caesars. Augustus himself, the first of the Roman emperors, is sometimes credited with its invention. Nero practiced it, as he wrote poetry, as a relaxation from the more serious pursuits of lust, incendiarism, and gluttony. But the greatest pantomimes—the name in Ancient Rome denoted the performers, and not the art of which they were the exponents—gave their whole lives to acting in dumb show, till they had mastered the last potentialities of expression in movement and gesture.

When Christianity triumphed, the pantomimes fled. Their favorite subjects were too frankly physical for the Fathers of the Church, and they were not sufficiently adaptable to seek new ones in the shadow of the Cross. But the subjects were there, had they realized it. Chaplin showed that in *The Pilgrim*. You remember the sequence in which, as an escaped convict disguised in clerical attire, he finds himself in the pulpit and tells the story of David and Goliath? It is a wonderful piece of miming, in which we follow every detail of the drama.

It was by accident that Chaplin rediscovered the art which, 1,900 years ago, cast its spell over the City of the Seven Hills. As a youth he was a member of a variety company touring the Channel Islands, home of a sturdy race to whom the King of England is still the Duke of Normandy. The islanders, speaking mainly the Norman-French patois of their ancestors, could not understand the Cockney phrases of the players, whose best jokes fell flat.

At last, in desperation, the company decided to try to get their effects by action and gesture. A single performance under the new conditions revealed Charles as a mime of genius and also showed him how powerful was the spell which this acting without words could cast over an audience. From that time he developed his natural gift for pantomimic expression and so unconsciously prepared himself for the day when the whole world should be his audience.

But the full flowering of his art came only after he was launched on his film career. He adapted his technique to the cinema and as he grew to appreciate at once the limitations and the possibilities of the screen, his mastery of the new mode of acting was perfected. He had realized that, as he himself had put it, "people can be moved more intensely by a gesture than by a voice."

American films generally were then in a highly favorable position. They were simpler, more direct than the best of the continental pictures, and consequently met the needs of a far wider audience. Had their producers and stars learned from Chaplin and the Europeans, the silent screen might have defined the talkies. The sound picture would have come just the same, but it would not have scooped the pool.

If we are ever to realize to the full the art of the cinema, I believe that it may be necessary deliberately to limit the mechanical aids we now employ so freely. I should like to see films without voices being made once more, but this time by producers who are alive to the potentialities of pantomime. Such pictures would be worth making, if only for this reason, that the audience for a talkie is necessarily limited by the factor of language, while the silent film can tell its story to the whole of the human race. Pantomime is the true universal tongue.

There are thousands of cinemas throughout the world which have never yet been wired for sound, and which constitute a market for nontalking pictures. Nor is it safe to assume that this is a shrinking market. There are many countries which lack the resources to make their own talkies. There are millions of people whose mother tongue will never be heard in any cinema and who understand thoroughly no other speech. As the standard of life rises throughout Asia and Africa, new cinemas will be built and a new film public will be created—a public which can be served most effectively by means of pantomime.

The English-speaking nations have here a great opportunity—and a great responsibility. The primitive mind thinks more easily in pictures than in words. The thing seen means more than the thing heard. The films which are shown amid the stillness of the African tropical night or under the skies of Asia may determine, in the long run, the fate of empires and of civilizations. They will promote, or destroy, the prestige by which the white man maintains his precarious supremacy amid the teeming multitudes of black and brown and yellow.

I hope that we shall not have to wait another four years for the next Chaplin picture. But it would be worth waiting for if he built up a team of actors and actresses who could use pantomime effectively. He has already shown his power of inspiring others by his production of *A Woman of Paris* and the grim realism with which the hardships of the Klondike pioneers were portrayed in *The Gold Rush*. And I see no reason why, if he can train such a company, he should not realize his ambition of playing the victor of Arcola. I think he might give us a picture of the young Napoleon that would be one of the most memorable things in the cinema.

Our difficulty in visualizing him in such a role is that we think of him as he appears on the screen. We think especially of his feet. Napoleon never had feet like that.

Neither has Chaplin. The feet are a "property"—the famous walk is the trick of a clever actor to suggest character and atmosphere. They are, in fact, the feet and walk of an ancient cabman, whom the youthful Charlie Chaplin encountered occasionally in the Kennington Road in London. To their original owner they were not at all humorous. But the boy saw the comic possibilities of that uneasy progress. He watched the old man and copied his movements until he had mastered every step in the dismal repertoire and turned it into mirth.

The same power of observation, the same patient thoroughness, could be used—and would be used—to give us convincing characterizations of serious roles. Charlie Chaplin's feet are not a handicap; they represent an asset—the power to convert the thing seen into the thing shown.

And the real Chaplin is a man of character and culture. As Sidney

Earle Chaplin put it, when interviewed at the tender age of five: "People get a wrong impression of Dad. It's not good style to throw pies, but he only does it in the films. He never throws pies at home."

I believe, therefore, that the future of Charlie Chaplin may lie mainly in the portrayal of serious roles in silent, or rather, nontalking films, and in the development of a universal cinema.

He need not ignore sound entirely. His pictures can be wedded to music. Natural sounds may be introduced. But these effects would be accessories only—the films could be shown—without any serious weakening of their appeal, in cinemas which were not wired for sound.

If Mr. Chaplin makes pictures of this kind, I think that he will not only increase his already great reputation, but he will blaze a trail which others will follow, and add enormously to the range of cinematic art.

It is a favorite cliché of film critics, in discussing talking pictures, to say that we cannot go back. In effect, they suggest that, because technical progress has given us sound, all films must be talkies and will continue to be so forever. Such statements reveal a radical misconception of the nature of progress and the nature of art. As well say that, because there is painting in oils, there must be no etchings; or that because speech is an integral part of a stage play, dialogue must be added to ballet. To explore the possibilities of the nontalking film, to make of it a new and individual art form, would not be a retrograde step, but an advance.

There are many brilliant and original minds associated with the cinema today. But there is no one so well equipped for this experiment as Mr. Chaplin. Possibly no one else would dare to make it.

I wish him good luck—and the courage of his own convictions and his own magnificent powers. But I hope also that he will not forget the world's need of laughter. Let him play in tragedy by all means. Let him display to us the full extent of his histrionic genius. But let him come back—at least occasionally—to the vein of comedy that has been the world's delight for twenty years.

A Reaction to the Praise Given Chaplin's Artistry

by GEORGE JEAN NATHAN

1. Charlie Chaplin is a superior clown.
2. Charlie Chaplin is the most famous product of the Hollywood studios.
3. Charlie Chaplin is an international favorite.
4. Charlie Chaplin often combines with his humor the effective touch of pathos.
5. Charlie Chaplin is one of the few really expert pantomimists that the screen has developed.

1. *True.*
2. *True.*
3. *True.*
4. *True.*
5. *True.*

1. Charlie Chaplin is a great artist.
2. Charlie Chaplin is a genius.
3. Charlie Chaplin is a great actor with infinite possibilities as a tragedian.
4. Charlie Chaplin is a great movie director.
5. Charlie Chaplin shows himself in the preparation of his pictures to be a highly imaginative scenarist and a skilful musician.

1. *Eliminate the adjective and heavily qualify the noun.*
2. *Bosh.*
3. *A limited actor with no possibilities as a tragedian.*
4. *Competent but certainly not great.*
5. *A sometimes moderately imaginative scenarist and a very shabby musician.*

From Passing Judgments by George Jean Nathan (New York: Alfred A. Knopf, Inc., 1934), pp. 210–14.

Now that we have had his picture, *City Lights,* believed by Chaplin himself to mark the pinnacle of his talents in the various directions above named, some such critical stock-taking of his gifts and resources may be undertaken. Since he devoted three solid years of effort to the picture, it may—even without Chaplin's word for it—be held as a standard of more or less final judgment. In what light does it disclose him? It discloses him as still the ingratiating clown with a comedy routine that remains exactly the same as that displayed in his very earliest pictures. Its humor, edited by him, consists chiefly in a series of ancient "gags," such as the jocosity implicit in a stab in the seat, in the eating of paper streamers under the impression that they are spaghetti, in the adjustment of the thumb to the nose, in the accidental falling backward into a body of water and splashing around therein, in an inopportune attack of hiccoughs (on this occasion embellished with a whistle), in the pursuit of a cigar butt, and in the propulsion from a house of an unwelcome guest at the point of a toe. Its musical accompaniment, save for a few moments' burlesque of the talking pictures, amounts to nothing more than a cheap paraphrase of such past popular tunes as "Valencia" and the like. And its remarkably original and imaginative thematic thread of pathos—so lavishly praised by the journalistic enthusiasts—is discovered to be the long familiar motif dear to Max Maurey's Grand Guignol and the sentimental novelists and playwrights of a bygone day: the blindness which imagines it beholds beauty and, with the return of vision, finds to its own and another's heartache only the commonplace and the sadly ugly.

Through all this, Chaplin moves as he has always, without much variation of any kind, moved. He is still the fundamentally proficient zany that he was years ago, but so inelastic is his technique that his every movement, every grimace, every gesture, every eye-lift is foretellable a second or two ahead of itself. Every now and then in his career—or at least since he abandoned the high silk hat he used in his first picture and put on the funny little derby—he has hit upon a jolly or tender bit of stage business that has lent to his performance a momentary superficial aspect of novelty. But, in the main, his antics, often winning though they are, have followed a more or less established pattern.

The funniest moment in *Easy Street* was not Chaplin's, but the scene wherein a monstrous thug, walking down the street with a girl after committing murder, arson, mayhem, and what not, suddenly reflects that he is walking on the wrong side of the lady and chevalier-like quickly changes his position. Certainly half the pathos touched with humor in *The Kid* was due to the performance in that picture of the then little Jackie Coogan. The monkeyshines of the fire department, rather than the tricks of Chaplin, constituted the most comical

Charlie Chaplin as The Tramp (*circa* 1915).

"The dance of Pan," *Modern Times* (1936); shot 81 of scenario, section V.

A posed shot on the elaborate set of *Modern Times* with Chester Conklin.

Jack Oakie, Charlie Chaplin, and Henry Daniell in *The Great Dictator* (1940).

The modern Bluebeard has troubles with a victim (Martha Raye) in *Monsieur Verdoux* (1947).

A struggle with Big Jim (Mack Swain) in *The Gold Rush* (1925).

Executing Harold Lloyd's "thrill comedy" in *The Circus* (1928). From The Museum of Modern Art/Film Stills Archive.

The Tramp in 1915 and a more sophisticated version in *City Lights* (1931).

Charlie conquers the villain (Eric Campbell) in *Easy Street* (1917).

A completely equipped soldier; a posed shot for *Shoulder Arms* (1918).

Chaplin directs *The Gold Rush* (1925) with Alf Reeves, Rollie Totheroth, and Charles Reisner.

Chaplin with Claire Bloom in *Limelight* (1952).

moments in *The Fireman,* and the audience's loud shouts of mirth over the spectacle of Chaplin hanging on to the hut toppling over the precipice in *The Gold Rush* were evoked not by Chaplin but by a hired dummy. It would be interesting for a better memory than mine to plumb the various films further and determine just how much of their real humor or pathos was directly attributable to Chaplin's performances or to those of others. What is to be credited to Chaplin as a scenario-compiler or a director is apparently not always properly to be credited to him as an actor.

In *City Lights,* Chaplin had a rich opportunity to make use of sounds, both for their own valuable collaborative effect and in the way of travesty, which he did not take advantage of. After the first few moments with their imitation of the talking screen's voices in terms of musical instruments—a fetching idea—there was no use of sound that was not stale and obvious. The imagination shown by René Clair, the French director, in *Under the Roofs of Paris,* in such a situation, say, as that wherein the increasing volume of an approaching train accompanies the mounting anger and desperate combat of the two gangsters, was nowhere visible in the Chaplin film. The musical invention and humor divulged by the director of such a German picture as *Two Hearts in Waltz Time* were completely absent, as was the murderous talking picture burlesque of even some such third-rate Mack Sennett film as *A Hollywood Hero.*

The newspaper hallelujah chorus, perhaps not altogether oblivious of the size of the advertisements and the consequent glee of the advertising departments, proclaimed *City Lights* and Chaplin—I quote literally—in the following terms: "superb," "incomparable, magnificent," "a dazzling pattern of comedy and pathos," "a great genius," "an artist without a peer," "killingly funny," "a very brilliant film," etc., etc. The picture and Chaplin were not any of these—and by a long shot. I should sum up the situation rather by saying that the picture was one of the poorest that Chaplin has made and that Chaplin himself, while still the best clown that the movies have bred, and while a pantomimist above the ordinary, is no longer, because of endless repetition, anything like so amusing as once he was. In plain fact, he is frequently a bore.

An Evaluation of Chaplin's Silent Comedy Films, 1916–36

by DONALD W. McCAFFREY

A giant step was taken by Chaplin when he produced twelve ex-
cellently conceived and executed two-reel works for Mutual Films in
1916 and 1917. It was his most fertile period and at least one minor
masterpiece, *Easy Street* (1917), sprang from this frenzy of creativity.
Some of the comedian's working methods, his faults and strengths
came into clear focus at this time. Many of his film's plots were
sketchy and erratic; such plots seemed to reflect many of the im-
promptu story-developing techniques of the Mack Sennett tradition.
One A.M. (1916), a *tour de force* of merit, proved successful completely on the strength of Chaplin's acrobatic skills and clever pantomime routines—the story line is slight. This work also shows one
of the comedian's methods of gathering material. In it he incorporated
material from the music-hall stage. *One A.M.* is an elaborate solo
routine that looks like a "turn" of a variety show merely photographed
on movie film. There was little of the film that could not be as
effectively presented on the stage. Only a few close-up reactions shots of
the little drunk struggling with stairs, stuffed animals, and a mechan-
ized folding bed showed the medium in operation. Chaplin the actor
dominated. The work's main fault lay in its repetition of the pratfall
(over twenty-five) and personal injury or discomfiture. Despite an attempt at variety, even Chaplin could not find enough different ways
to fall and sustain the piece.

Easy Street (1917) is the one exception in the body of twelve films
of this period. It is by far the best of the whole Mutual output because

Excerpted from Four Great Comedians: Chaplin, Lloyd, Keaton,
Langdon, *by Donald W. McCaffrey (London: A. Zwemmer Ltd.; New
York: A. S. Barnes & Company, Inc., 1968, pp. 31–50. Reprinted by
permission of The Tantivy Press, in association with A. Zwemmer
Ltd., and A. S. Barnes & Company, Inc.*

it has a strong dramatic story line fused with Chaplin's outstanding acting skills and ingenious gags. In this work he employed parallel plot lines with a finesse that he never completely equalled in his later efforts. Chaplin has not dipped into his background on the English stage for the routines in this film; the story is designed for the motion picture. The film has a tale that is vigorously told; it holds interest with the little fellow turned policeman and shows his conflict with a brute of a man (played broadly by Eric Campbell) and his gang of thugs. Chaplin tells his story directly and acts with economy—two virtues which are not always seen in his films. If the comedian had ceased his work for the silent screen and returned to the English music halls, he would still have a place in the sun with *Easy Street*.

Chaplin moved on and created another short, masterfully executed work, *Shoulder Arms*, in 1918. This excellent spoof of the trials of a doughboy of World War I is replete with well-conceived comic invention. Chaplin has a brilliantly clever slapstick scene showing his little tramp disguised as a tree as he spies for U.S. forces in enemy territory. Detected by the enemy, he plays a frantic game of hide-and-seek with a German soldier in a wood with trees that are similar in shape to his disguise. He periodically freezes and assumes poses which match the trees around him in order to outsmart his pursuer; then he runs wildly when the soldier stabs a nearby tree with his bayonet. Full of ingenious gags, this comic chase not only outstripped Chaplin's competitor Mack Sennett; it is a chase which will match and generally exceed in quality anything of this nature today. But the structural fault mars the work. Especially disappointing is the cliché dream ending—that is, all the exploits of the little soldier behind enemy lines are merely a figment of his nightmare.

When Chaplin started producing feature-length works in 1921 with his famous *The Kid*, even more pronounced weaknesses in the dramatic story line resulted. A detailed scenario of this work which I have developed for my studies reveals many structural faults. A film that used fifteen sequences, of which the first three sequences and number fourteen have marked defects, the work has a typical crudity of storytelling that Chaplin never was able to erase in his feature works. Laboriously, he began his story with a sequence of direct, serious (and unfortunately), overdrawn, uninspired exposition. Even banal titling encroaches on this part of the film. An unwed mother is introduced with the title "A young girl . . . her mistake is that she is a mother." [1] As if under the influence of the German cinema

---

[1] John Montgomery and Theodore Huff have quoted this line: "Her only sin was motherhood." Two prints viewed by the editor displayed the title given in the above text. At times titles were changed when films were reissued. Only when the original release print can be identified will the correct version be verified.

of the time, Chaplin comments on the suffering of the young woman by interjecting a still picture of Christ bearing the cross up a hill. Throughout the first three sequences, the serious elements which Chaplin uses to sustain a feature-length work are driven home with sledgehammer blows.

In sequence fourteen, a portion of *The Kid* which is nearly six minutes long, Chaplin also mars the work by presenting an elaborate, tangential dream episode. Both damned and justified by the critics, this portion of the film received a largely negative vote. Film historians Maurice Bardeche and Robert Brasillach, for example, found this sequence a good illustration of Chaplin's tendency to insert episodes which have little bearing on the main plot.[2] Chaplin himself reports that playwright James M. Barrie found the dream portion of the film superfluous.

Sequence fifteen also mars the work. Like Chaplin's later work, *The Gold Rush* (1925), the film exhibits a forced happy ending which shows the little tramp being taken by the police to rejoin the Kid and to meet the child's mother. The swiftness of this resolution is less at fault than the trite material and the awkward handling of the situation by Chaplin. Visually (both in pantomime and camera work) the conclusion is banal—unworthy of the amount of praise that some critics have given this short sequence. Parker Tyler, in an unusual and, one is forced to conclude, ridiculous symbolic analysis, sees the car that takes Charlie to the Kid and the mother as the "magic vehicle that restores order." [3] Gilbert Seldes, champion of the popular arts, misfires in his analysis of this last scene by effusively writing:

> He is ushered into a limousine instead of a patrol wagon—it is the beginning of the happy ending. And as the motor starts he flashes at the spectators of his felicity a look of indescribable poignancy. It is frightened, it is hopeful, bewildered; it lasts a fraction of a second and is blurred by the plate glass of the car. I cannot hope to set down the qualities of it, how it becomes a moment of unbearable intensity, and how one is breathless with suspense—and with adoration.[4]

Such a reading of this incident seems to be merely Seldes' interpolation. I have looked carefully at the action which Seldes describes

[2] Maurice Bardeche and Robert Brasillach, *The History of Motion Pictures,* trans. Iris Barry (New York: W. W. Norton and Co., 1938), p. 215.

[3] Parker Tyler, *Chaplin: Last of the Clowns* (New York: The Vanguard Press, Inc., 1948), p. 112.

[4] Gilbert Seldes, *The Seven Lively Arts* (New York: Sagamore Press, Inc., 1957), p. 46.

and find that only a comic "take" expression of puzzlement exists
on Chaplin's face. No close-up is given which would reveal the
poignancy which the critic finds in this scene. This is, I believe, a
case in which a film-editing viewer exposes some of the rhapsodic writings which have often been developed when an impressed critic has reflected on Chaplin's works.

Such enthusiastic praise from evaluators who viewed *The Kid* can
be understood when the virtues of the work are set forth. My dissection
of this film could not pale my feelings for the little tramp and his
love for the little "orphan" that he takes under his wing. Moments of
tenderness when the frail, lonely tramp embraces the Kid have all
the strength and sentiment of a Dickens story brought to life. A depth
of comic character that is only faintly seen in most film comedies of
today is evident. Serious moments between the Kid and the little tramp
illustrate the outstanding features of his films—the creation of sympathy for his characters which some critics view as the "profound" in
Chaplin. Better than he had ever done before, Chaplin displayed a
clown who could exibit the slapstick of Harlequin with the moon-
struck sadness of Pierrot. The fusion of these trites was not complete,
however, until Chaplin had created *The Gold Rush* in 1925.

Far greater skill in story construction was exhibited by Chaplin's
formidable competitor, Harold Lloyd, who created his first feature
work, *Grandma's Boy*, in 1922, just a year after Chaplin released
The Kid. This new work even impressed Chaplin, who was not prone
to praise his rivals. The creator of the little tramp was reported to
have written Lloyd that *Grandma's Boy* was an inspiration to him to
do his best work and "to be contented with nothing else but the best
for himself." [5] While Lloyd's work had some weaknesses—its seven-
teen sequences were rather choppy in transitional phases, and the
climactic fight sequence was somewhat anticlimactic after a brilliant
chase sequence—the film was unified by a strong central comic idea
that resulted from the action of a clear-cut portrayal of a shy, small-
town boy. Chaplin's character in *The Kid* was rather vague at times—
an enigma and an erratic character who spasmodically took action to
solve his problems.

In 1924 Buster Keaton's *Sherlock Jr.*, a five-reel feature, exhibited a
clever, intricate, smoothly unified story line which made Chaplin's
The Kid and his three-reel 1923 production, *The Pilgrim*, seem
primitive. Storywise, Chaplin's works in the first part of the twenties
seemed to be fumbling throwbacks to the one- and two-reel comedies
of the formative age of the silent-screen comedy. Only Chaplin's acting

[5] John Montgomery, *Comedy Films* (London: George Allen Unwin Ltd., 1954),
p. 126.

skill and comic ingenuity pulled his works above those of the minor comedians of the times. The key scene in *The Pilgrim* that brought kudos from the critics was the comedian's pantomimed sermon on David and Goliath. A condensed version of my scenario for this three-reel work indicates Chaplin's acting skills:

> Charlie as the bogus minister opens the Bible on the podium, comes forward, and says: "I am going to tell you about David and Goliath . . ." (Title 16). He stretches his hand as high as possible and declares: "Goliath was a very tall man . . ." (Title 17). Charlie now takes a strong-man pose and feels his own muscle; he indicates a huge, flowing mustache and flourishes a sword. He moves back and looks into the Bible—then back toward the audience, he stoops over and indicates the size of David—about two feet off the floor. He snaps back into the strong-man pose and swings a sword. Menacingly he looks down and right. He switches to the David character who is looking up and left. David is pantomimed picking up a stone in a sling and throwing it. The stone is shown by gesticulation as going into the forehead of the giant and plopping out behind. Goliath falls. David is shown cutting off the giant's head and putting it on the end of the sword. The head is then thrown off nonchalantly over the shoulder and given a little Chaplinesque back-kick without looking back. (Chaplin often used this trick with a discarded cigarette.) The little tramp has finished the story; he executes a delicate Frenchlike bow to the left and right and goes off behind the choir box in a run. A little boy claps in the audience. Charlie enters again and bows—runs off left again. He comes back in a flourish and throws kisses to the congregation—opens his arms broadly and clasps his hands together in a victorious salute to himself.

This routine is a brilliant piece of work; Chaplin's sense of timing was never better, his footwork never keener. So, despite weaknesses of the total work, the comedian's genius reigns in such a moment.

The Pilgrim is also interesting because it shows Chaplin using a touch of genteel comedy material. Much of the comedy evolves from the bogus minister's embarrassments when he reverts to his old ways before stuffy, small-town people. These people find that their new minister often conducts himself in a worldly way. In the scene described above only a small boy claps at the little tramp's performance; the rest of the congregation are horrified by his theatrics. The parlor scene and eating scene in which he is an invited guest at a Sunday noon meal also rely on the humor of embarrassment. Thus, in this film, his humor more nearly approaches that used by Harold Lloyd in many of the early scenes of *Grandma's Boy*. This was Chaplin's only experiment with this type of material. He could not handle it as effectively as his competitors.

In 1925, however, Chaplin reached a peak with his skilled blend of the serious and the comic in *The Gold Rush*. His virtues finally over-balanced his faults. Some of the golden moments of silent-screen comedy were created in this work. Stranded in a small cabin during a blizzard in the Yukon, the little tramp was forced by hunger to eat his own shoe. For this bizarre Thanksgiving dinner, Chaplin's skill in comic invention came into full play. The starved, weary little fellow carved and ate parts of his shoe as if it were turkey. A bent nail from the shoe became a wishbone; and, by an incongruous turn of the little tramp's mind, a side dish on which he had deposited the shoestrings was transformed into a plate of spaghetti. He consequently wound the shoestrings around his fork and devoured them with the air of a gourmet. Such comic transposition was Chaplin's forte, and the critics who viewed the film found that such invention would "ring the bell." [6] Many evaluators of his work since the first showing of the film have found this scene one of their favorites.

In delicate, facile pantomime *The Gold Rush* had no equal. Fur-thermore, many of the actions of the little tramp when he was starv-ing had a unique blend of the serious and the comic which were rooted in the character of the lonely little soul. With great pantomimic skill, Chaplin portrayed the hollow-eyed comic hero, eyeing the stub of a candle. Sadly the little tramp picked it up and nibbled it with rabbit bites—as if the candle were a piece of carrot or celery. And with a deft touch that showed Chaplin's genius, the little fellow sprinkled salt on this morsel of wax, found that it tasted better, and popped it into his mouth. With such actions a new depth in comic character was added, a dimension that was to make Chaplin the darling of the critics. The comedian was able to make us laugh and still feel sorry for this pathetic little man. The twentieth century, after *The Gold Rush*, seemed to house the reincarnation of the famous eighteenth-century French clown, Jean-Gaspard Deburau, a renowned Pierrot, blended with all the rollicking good spirit of the Clown created by the English music hall's favorite comedian, Gri-maldi.

While individual scenes were highly inventive and Chaplin's acting was at a high peak, there were some structural faults in *The Gold Rush*. While fewer sequences in the film (nine instead of the fifteen in *The Kid*) seemed to tighten the story line, overdrawn exposition de-veloped in the comedy when Chaplin introduced the love interest in

---

[6] Review of *The Gold Rush*, *Variety*, 79 (1 July 1925), 32.

sequences that take up twenty minutes running time of the film. The struggles for survival in a remote cabin had already developed lively comedy—nearly three reels of comedy had gone by. A serious, pathetic love attachment then developed when the little tramp saw a beautiful dance-hall girl. It took some effort for Chaplin to return to effective comic episodes, and he needed to get his little tramp back into the wilderness in order to increase the pace and interest in the story.

While Chaplin's use of the motion-picture medium generally is very weak, he is able to create excitement in a literal cliff-hanging climactic sequence. The little tramp and his friend Big Jim McKay are shown caught in a rustic cabin that slips and clings miraculously to the edge of a precipice by a single rope wedged between two rocks and attached to the dwelling. Both Charlie and Big Jim are thrown onto the floor of the dwelling that tilts at an angle of over 35 degrees. With anguished, perplexed faces, they look up the floor and wonder how they can climb up without the whole cabin slipping into the abyss. The medium takes over: editing, contrasting shots, titles, and special effects help create the comic horror that has been thrust upon the two men. The slipping of the cabin is emphasized by a miniature cabin and cliff—a product of the special-effects department.

Short in duration, the shots assist in emphasizing the dangerous situation. When Big Jim has hoisted his huge frame on the top of the hapless little tramp, he is able to get out the front door of the cabin. Left alone, poor Charlie doesn't realize that Big Jim has found gold at the edge of the cliff and has forgotten his plight. His cries of help cause the cabin to inch down. Finally Big Jim heeds the cries and throws a rope to the little fellow. A process shot shows Charlie coming out of the front door just as the cabin (in miniature) plunges over the edge and into the abyss.

The miniature work coupled with the process shots help greatly to convey the action and develop the comedy. Unfortunately these special effects are rather crude and fall into the same class as the rather poor exterior scenes of the Yukon Territory. There is too much papier-mâché and too many poorly painted sets for a film of 1925. Despite this weakness, Chaplin edits this sequence with considerable skill and shows that when he deals with spectacular scenes he can use the medium to assist a comic situation.

While structural defects and use of the medium seemed to be overlooked by the critics of the film, many evaluators recognized faults in the prolonged resolution of *The Gold Rush*. Theodore Huff felt that the conclusion of the work changed the total "mood" of the film drama by incorporating a happy ending.[7] Robert Payne believed

[7] Theodore Huff, *Charlie Chaplin* (New York: Henry Schuman, 1951), p. 188.

that such an ending was a serious weakness that marred the work because the union of the little tramp and the girl was an improbable resolution.[8] That is, such a union was not consistent with the bent of the
characters. I concur with these views after an examination of the film.
As in *The Kid*, Chaplin has created a lost soul on the fringe of society
who is doomed to loneliness. Too much of the ostracized, pathetic
Pierrot exists in his comic character to allow a happy ending. Chaplin
does not make this mistake in *The Circus*.

Chaplin's last work in the twenties was created in 1928. While
The Circus is today one of his least-known films, the picture did reveal one of his most poignant moments. A happy ending (which
seemed so illogical in *The Kid* and *The Gold Rush*) was avoided. The
little tramp was left alone—alone and apart from the circus that had
afforded him a taste of fame and excitement. A rival got the girl he
loved, and the childlike little man was shown viewing the long line
of circus wagons moving away from him as he leaned sadly on his cane
in the harsh early-morning sunlight. Chaplin underacted this moment
with great skill—suggesting more than he revealed. This glimpse of
the sad clown, like other glimpses in the total film, revealed a poetic
touch which raised Chaplin's works to a meritorious level. A less successful scene, yet highly poignant moment, was created in *The Gold
Rush*—but it is more stagy and contrived. Chaplin showed his rejected
little fellow looking into a dance-hall window, viewing others in the
merriment of a New Year's celebration. These two moments in the
films provide a key to the understanding of Chaplin's distinguishing
characteristic: he was able to create a comedy which effectively blended
serious elements with the comic. His rivals were never as successful
when they used the same kind of material. Harold Lloyd, for example,
tried to promote sympathy for his comic country lad in *Grandma's
Boy* and his naive, young social climber in *The Freshman*. But Lloyd
overplayed the moments in which he might have given dimension to
his character by this method, and as a result, sometimes produced
rather shallow serious scenes.

Compared with *The Gold Rush*, *The Circus* does not incorporate as
much serious material. When the work was reviewed, Robert Sherwood was the only major movie critic who hailed Chaplin's return to
stronger, more elaborate comedy scenes. Sherwood felt that his use of
rollicking, lively comedy material of his early one- and two-reel works
was the essence of the best Chaplin.[9] There was merit in this view.
Many of Chaplin's great acting skills and ingenious gags were created
in the gay, nearly irascible, nose-thumbing spirit of his earlier works.

---

[8] Robert Payne, *The Great God Pan* (New York: Hermitage House, 1952), p. 204.
[9] Robert Sherwood, Review of *The Circus*, *Life*, 91 (26 January 1928), 26.

His use of the lonely soul is his distinctive feature, but it is only part of the total character. My detailed examination of and conclusion concerning the total film reveal, however, a fault that seemed to be overlooked by Sherwood. While *The Gold Rush* became a unified work by showing the tramp's struggle against a hostile environment, no clear, unifying conflict or idea exists in *The Circus*—the story line becomes an erratic adventure of a little tramp among circus people. A villainous, exploiting circus manager was a foil for Charlie. This antagonist remained a cliché; he did not have the delightful comic exaggeration of the bullies that inhabited Chaplin's early works. It would seem that Chaplin expected us to take his villain seriously, but we find this pale refugee from the nineteenth-century melodrama (possessing the black hat, black handlebar mustache, and black heart) a bore after witnessing the antics of the brawny, bearlike villain of *The Gold Rush*.

Making the same error as he did in *The Kid*, Chaplin opened *The Circus* on a serious note that was unimaginative and heavy-handed. When the little tramp was introduced in a lively chase sequence with a pickpocket, the comic story line began to sparkle.

It should be noted that in this neglected work there are many laughable scenes that are worthy of Chaplin. His comic pantomime is nimble and suave. While it may be classified as an uneven work with many faults, it is by far a greater work than the much-applauded first feature, *The Kid*. Even though the nine sequences of this work are not ostensibly tied together with a strong, clear-cut comic idea, it is still an adventure that holds the attention of an audience viewing the work today.

In *The Circus* Chaplin also created many clever comic scenes which surpassed those of his earlier works. The little tramp's feeble attempts to be a clown in a circus produced ingenious comedy which revealed an inept little fellow who was most funny when he made mistakes in executing his clown routines. Combining great danger with his comedy in a fashion which probably reflected the influence of Harold Lloyd's *Safety Last*, Chaplin showed his comic character trying to escape from the cage of a sleeping lion in which he had been accidentally trapped; and the little fellow executed comical, involuntary arabesques on a high wire when he was forced into substituting for the star performer. Such situations encompass some of the most laughable moments in Chaplin's works.

With the coming of sound in the final years of the twenties, Chaplin's *The Circus* concluded his efforts in silent-screen drama. Even though *City Lights* in 1931 used no human speech, music and sound effects on the sound track were evidence that the comedian was stubbornly being dragged into the world of sound from the marvelous world of silence. It was in this land of black and white—shadows and light—that Chaplin created some of his best work. Each of the features being examined in this study shows the treatment of its story material using sweeping, sentimental strokes. Unlike the other comedians of the twenties, Chaplin was a sentimentalist and a romanticist. Comedians Lloyd, Keaton, and Langdon experimented with comic versions of the struggles of a little man—a little man who seemed to be a comic counterpart of the Horatio Alger, Jr. hero—a simple, honest young man who becomes a success. Chaplin avoided this material, generally, even though his tacked-on happy endings seemed to be influenced by such subject matter. *The Kid*, with slight updating, seemed like a variation on a Charles Dickens novel; *The Circus* had material akin to the struggles of Pierrot with the juxtapositioning of Harlequinlike slapstick; and *The Gold Rush*, seemingly less distant and very specific, still had material treated with broad strokes and abstracted from reality through Chaplin's romanticism.

Several major conclusions may be drawn from the foregoing discussion. Chaplin's works are marked by strong assets and deficits. One of his greatest faults lies in his awkward storytelling. His greatest virtues, his acting skill and his comic invention, however, made him the master of silent-screen pantomiming.

My analysis also leads me to the conclusion that *The Gold Rush*, with all its faults, is superior to the other two features which have been discussed. It achieves a higher degree of unity by using the strong central idea of the frail tramp struggling against great odds on the Alaskan frontier. A reversal of roles and a burlesque treatment of the adventures of the wild northland seem to operate to achieve the comic in this work. Among rugged "he-men" of the Yukon, the little tramp cuts a laughable figure as he weakly faces storms, men crazy for gold, and starvation.

The failure to unify his works, however, is evident in his other films of the twenties—not only his features but his one- to three-reel works. I believe that a close investigation of his works will expose this weakness. I find the works of Harold Lloyd, Buster Keaton, and Harry Langdon much better than Chaplin's in this respect; they were much better storytellers. Lloyd achieved unity through strong central comic ideas in three of his famous works: *Grandma's Boy* (1922), *Safety Last* (1923), and *The Freshman* (1926). Keaton's *Sherlock Jr.* (1924), and Langdon's *Long Pants* (1927) were unified in the same way and exhibited a tightness of solid continuity that was lacking in Chaplin's films.

While this study concentrates on the comic films of the twenties, that era which has been called the golden age of comedy, it cannot overlook Chaplin's later works. He attempted to continue the silent-screen tradition into the formative period of the sound film. At least one more masterpiece, *City Lights*, came from the famous comedian's effort to continue his work in the older mode. Essentially this 1931 film was a silent picture created in the infant years of the "talkies." Chaplin was warned of the financial risk—that people wanted films with spoken dialogue. Nevertheless, he used merely a musical score and limited sound effects for the sound track of the film. This was, therefore, a silent movie. Many silent filmmakers from the 1910s on, usually producers of high-budgeted features with major directors and actors, sent prepared scores with the films that were rented by movie theaters throughout the country.

Despite the lack of human voice, few people objected; *City Lights* made a profit of five million dollars. And rightly so; it was a critical success. In many ways this film is the equal of *The Gold Rush*. With fewer weaknesses in story line than Chaplin's 1928 *The Circus*, it achieved unity by using a central comic idea in the manner of *The Gold Rush*.

While *City Lights* has the initial look of a contemporary film on a contemporary subject, it is not. The romantic-sentimental spirit of Chaplin's main body of work is revealed. The big city seems like a far-off place—somewhere in Europe, possibly. The home of the blind girl, Virginia Cherrill's role, has the look of a poor Spanish court-yard and is reached by an archway from the city streets. In short, the environment is a synthesis that suited Chaplin's romantic view. The work is subtitled "A Comedy Romance in Pantomime." There is a unique juxtapositioning of pathos and knockout farce in the film that has made it a favorite of many critics. There is a clumsiness in the structure of the work that is disconcerting; the pace of the work some-times becomes overly slow as transitional scenes focusing on the blind girl's plight are used between fast-moving comedy scenes.

Some of Chaplin's innovations in comedy are revealed when the lit-tle tramp is befriended by a drunk millionaire. At a nightclub the ine-briated Charlie mistakes an apache dance for the real thing and tries to save the girl from what he believes is a dreadful mauling by a Parisian rowdy. As he eats spaghetti, the celebrating crowd throws confetti and a streamer of the paper lands in his plate; unaware, drunkenly concentrating on his eating, he chews away on the paper as if it were a very long piece of spaghetti—rising from his chair, stretching and nibbling as if he seems headed toward the ceiling.

By far the most laughable scene occurs when Charlie takes the desperation step to provide money for the blind girl. Chaplin revives and refurbishes material from his 1914 *The Knockout*, and his 1915 *The Champion*. Forced into a quick-money scheme, he finds himself fighting in the ring with a person of superior ability. Realizing his inferiority, Charlie does not play the game; he avoids the prize fighter by his dancelike, ring-around-the-rosy effort, keeping the referee between the brutal pugilist and himself. The whole sequence is lively, colorful, and extremely funny.

A sequence preceding this portion of the film shows some of the older, cruder forms of humor being employed. Charlie tries to make friends with his opponent in the locker room. His overtures are delicate and effete. He smiles and twists his head coyly, grasping his own knees with his hands in a childlike gesture of friendship. The tough, apelike boxers around him are appalled. His opponent retreats into a curtained room to change into his boxing trunks. Homosexuality as material for humor, therefore, was used in an age when it was a taboo. But Chaplin's skill was great, and he was able to execute the gag with finesse and make it acceptable.

And finally, the "pathos" which Chaplin employed reached its greatest height. Theodore Huff aptly describes the quality of the last scene of the movie:

> The equivocal ending of the film, ironic and vibrant with the tragic sense of life, seldom fails to bring tears. The terrified smile of the tramp at the girl who has recovered her vision through him, and through that recovery is lost to him, is one of the most poignant scenes ever photographed.[10]

At this moment the dialogue used in the titles is effectively simple, and the power of understatement contrasts with the visual:

"You can see now?"

"Yes, I can see now."

And this is the end. The little tramp's smile is strangely twisted; his fingers and the rose she has given him touch the edge of the Pierrot mask.

Chaplin's next film, *Modern Times* (1936), was the comedian's last attempt to retain the silent-film tradition. A few concessions were made to the sound film; he allowed the sound of the human voice over a television set (a factory's closed-circuit TV system was employed comically—as in George Orwell's *1984* "Big Brother is watching you" television device). And Chaplin permitted the human voice for a radio and a record player. Finally, his most interesting concession: for one routine in the last portion of the film, Chaplin sang.

This work sums up all the comedian's virtues and faults. One of the last bursts of Chaplin's great comic invention and acting skill, *Modern Times* is an anthology with many of the comedian's old gags

---

[10] Huff, p. 226.

refurbished. We see him battling with cops and stuffed shirts as he did in his Essanay and Mutual two-reelers; he confronts both bullies and gentle people, as in his feature works of the twenties. He shows he can fight with amazing footwork, roller-skate with comic dignity, and juggle a tray laden with a mountain of food as he encounters drunks and dancers. And the man-child is also capable of falling in love. While many critics see the comedian engaging in strong satire, they fail to note the emphasis on warmth and gaiety in his fun-making. Chaplin is at his best when he burlesques the factory worker turned into a trained ape; he is at his best when he gathers his shabby dignity and confronts authority with the best air a little man can muster. Also we see the very human tenderness of the tramp who looks for a kind gesture in a cold, self-centered world. Episodic and meandering in its story line, *Modern Times* had dramatic weaknesses that tainted the total work, but the human figure of the little tramp never glowed brighter.

While critics have overlooked some of Chaplin's faults, their praise of his acting skill and his comic invention is generally sound. Chaplin was a master at both broad, acrobatic pantomime and simple routines that demanded slight hand movements and facial expressions. He was able to make smoking a cigarette and counting money extremely funny—slight things to be sure, but he firmly based his comedy on the eccentricities of the little tramp. His comic invention sprang from the unusual way this clown faced the world—whether it was battling a bully or spreading butter on his pancakes. Furthermore, Chaplin had an acting intensity that was unique. He seemed to believe in his little tramp and to become so much a part of the strange world he created for the character that almost everyone believed (and still does) that it could hardly be an actor playing the role. In fact, he became so identified with the role that many of his fans and the critics were disappointed with his sophisticated comic character, Henri Verdoux, in the 1947 film, *Monsieur Verdoux.*

The world of silence was Chaplin's medium. There were many moments in *The Great Dictator* (1940), *Monsieur Verdoux,* and *Limelight* (1953) that were worthy of Chaplin's genius. To me, however, his last great work was *Modern Times* in 1936. His little tramp remained in the world of silence—except for a song in the latter portion of the film. A new dimension was added to the little fellow—one that had never been seen before. The little tramp, the entertainer, was revealed. He danced and broke into a gay, charming song:

> El pwu el se domtroco
> La spinach or la tuko
> Cigaretto toto torlo

E rusho spagaletto
Senora ce la tima
Voulez vous la taxi meter
Le jonta tu la zita
Je le tu le tu le twaa
La der la ser pawnbroker
Lusern apprer how mucher
E se confess a potcha
Ponka walla ponka wa.[11]

It was a swan song; only a faint image of the tramp-clown existed in Chaplin's films from then on. The little tramp, urging his girl to smile and face a new dawn, walked down the road at the end of the film for the last time. A very human, warm little fellow that we all loved so well disappeared as he shuffled toward far-off hills.

[11] First words spoken by Chaplin for the film as recorded in review of *Modern Times, Stage,* March 1937, p. 72. The comedian's pantomime and vocal inflection help make sense of this manufactured language—a whimsey of Chaplin's creation.

REVIEWS

Impressions of Two Early Comedy Films

LOUIS DELLUC

◆◇◆

Easy Street

Charlie is roused from his open-air nap by the heavenly voices of the Hope Mission—preaching, harmonium, hymns, all complete. And still in a torpid state he goes inside, to get warm, or to pass the time, or for no reason at all. The stout lady lends him her hymnbook. His other neighbor hands him a baby. The pastor, thin and white and with frock coat on his body and his soul, talks and talks and talks. And everyone bawls to the greater glory of God. Heaven and all the angels visit Charlie the vagabond. Hosannah! It's restful here. And boring.

But—but the pastor's daughter turns round. Up to now she has presided over the harmonium and was only a back offered to divine service. And now, lo and behold! it's Edna—with such eyes and such hair and such lips. Charlie has found his road to Damascus. The pastor goes on desperately trying to convert him. Go on talking, go on: it doesn't need any effort not to listen to *him*. Edna smiles. Summits of rapture! theological and human, joys of this life and the life everlasting. And off goes Charlie on a crusade of life. He delivers up to the pastor the collection box full of pence, which he had appropriated— quite mechanically. He flings himself into the battle. Well, at least he opens the door and goes away.

The pointing finger of the Lord brings him to a police office in need of men. After a few minutes of very natural hesitation, quite comprehensible, he joins up, and here he is decked out in the sacred uniform of the police. The finger of the Lord, with unfailing accuracy in these things, puts him on duty in Easy Street, a regular cutthroat place, where rules the great ogre who keeps the district in terror. But little Charlie's ruse will get the better of the brute giant—thanks to an

From Charlie Chaplin *by Louis Delluc, translated by Hamish Miles* (*London: The Bodley Head, 1922*), *pp. 87–89, 93–95.*

alarmingly supple lamp post. Missiles fly from one window to another; there's a grand chain of murderers whirling about this street of tragedy and hysteria; the regular police don't steer clear of it all. And Charlie triumphs.

And the upshot of it all is that the low street becomes respectable; the notorious public house makes room for the New Mission; and the great ogre himself, in top hat and flowered waistcoat, takes his lady to service; the lamp posts never again suffer from giddiness, and Charlie, with correct and military air, the complete man of the world, offers his arm (yes, he knows which, already) to the buxom Edna, who was, is now, and ever shall be his guardian angel.

Shoulder Arms

In spite of all the people who take literature seriously (and even take only that seriously), I prefer Chaplin's *Shoulder Arms* to Barbusse's *Under Fire,* and to his imitators, and to the *J'Accuse* film. *Shoulder Arms* doesn't bombard anything and doesn't accuse anybody, but it is much more relentless.

The sufferings of the American Sammy doing his training and dreaming of the glorious trenches are explored without any romantic feeling or any preaching. Irony is far stronger than sermonizing. And humor is a wonderful thing: it has irony in it, and many other ingredients too. This little cinematographic picture is one of the most truthful that the War inspired in any peace-loving man. The farcical atmosphere of the film, its amusing details and jokes, its scenario on the lines of a sketch, only accentuate the cruel satire of the fantasy. It never declaims, not even against declaiming.

The docility of the wretched private calls down the thunders of the NCO (whence the malicious cruelty of useless parades). And then —"*Dismiss!*" and Charlie flings himself down on his bed and sleeps like a child. His dream transports him to the French front. Those barbed early days in the line! The first shell, the first showers of rain, the first enthusiasm to be a hero. The letter which doesn't arrive is an exquisite episode in the manner of *The Vagabond* and *A Dog's Life.* Charlie is touching there. And the night in the flooded dugout is a bold stroke of stage-setting. There you have burlesque taking a completely new guise. It is there that people who have no real sensitiveness will be bored: they will find "nothing very much to laugh at." Dinner and the cigarette, the helmet that won't keep on, the infantry attack, and the patrol where Charlie is camouflaged as a tree trunk, have all got power. And the gaiety becomes splendid clowning with that delightful adventure when Charlie captures the Kaiser, the

Crown Prince, and Hindenburg and brings them all back into the American lines.

This film justifies all that one can expect from the cinema.

There we are really in a country which is splendidly illimitable. And moreover we have Chaplin, who by force of his personal genius, is something above the art of the cinema. We should never have dared to hope so much from it.

And shall I astonish Forbes Robertson much by telling him that Charlie Chaplin is a Shakespearean actor?

An Early, Detailed Account of the Action in The Pawnshop

GILBERT SELDES

❖◈◈❖

"The egregious merit of Chaplin," says T. S. Eliot, "is that he has escaped in his own way from the realism of the cinema and invented a *rhythm*. Of course the unexplored opportunities of the cinema for eluding realism must be very great."

It amused me once, after seeing *The Pawnshop,* to write down exactly what had happened. Later I checked up the list, and I print it here. I believe that Chaplin is so great on the screen, his effect so complete, that few people are aware, afterward, of how much he has done. Nor can they be aware of how much of Chaplin's work is "in his own way"—even when he does something which another could have done he adds to it a touch of his own. I do not pretend that the following analysis is funny; it may be useful:

Charlot enters the pawnshop; it is evident that he is late. He com-

From The Seven Lively Arts *by Gilbert Seldes (New York: Harper & Row, Publishers, Inc., 1924), Appendix, pp. 361–64. Copyright, 1924 by Harper & Row, Publishers, Inc.; renewed, 1952 by Gilbert Seldes. Reprinted by permission of the publisher. This kind of objective, detailed, descriptive analysis was rare in the mid-twenties.*

pares his watch with the calendar pad hanging on the wall, and hastily begins to make up for lost time by entering the back room and going busily to work. He takes a duster out of a valise and meticulously dusts his walking stick. Then proceeding to other objects, he fills the room with clouds of dust, and when he begins to dust the electric fan, looking at something else, the feathers are blown all over the room. He turns and sees the plucked butt of the duster—and carefully puts it away for tomorrow.

With the other assistant he takes a ladder and a bucket of water and goes out to polish the three balls and the shop sign. After some horseplay he rises to the top of the ladder and reaches over to polish the sign; the ladder sways, teeters, with Charlot on top of it. A policeman down the street looks aghast, and sways sympathetically with the ladder. Yet struggling to keep his balance, Charlot is intent on his work, and every time the ladder brings him near the sign he dabs frantically at it until he falls.

A quarrel with his fellow worker follows. The man is caught between the rungs of the ladder, his arms imprisoned. Charlot calls a boy over to hold the other end of the ladder and begins a boxing match. Although his adversary is incapable of moving his arms, Charlot sidesteps, feints, and guards, leaping nimbly away from imaginary blows. The policeman interferes and both assistants run into the shop. By a toss of a coin Charlot is compelled to go back to fetch the bucket. He tiptoes behind the policeman, snatches the bucket, and with a wide swing and a swirling motion evades the policeman and returns. He is then caught by the boss in another fight and is discharged.

He makes a tragic appeal to be reinstated. He says he has eleven children, so high, and so high, and so high—until the fourth one is about a foot taller than himself. The boss relents only as Charlot's stricken figure is at the door. As he is pardoned, Charlot leaps upon the old boss, twining his legs around his abdomen; he is thrown off and surreptitiously kisses the old man's hand. He goes into the kitchen to help the daughter and passes dishes through the clothes wringer to dry them—passes a cup twice, as it seems not to be dry the first time. Then his hands. The jealous assistant provokes a fight; Charlot has a handful of dough and is about to throw it when the boss appears. With the same motion Charlot flings the dough into the wringer, passes it through as a pie crust, seizes a pie plate, trims the crust over it, and goes out to work.

At the pawnshop counter pass a variety of human beings. Charlot is taken in by a sob story about a wedding ring; he tries to test the genuineness of goldfish by dropping acid on them. Sent to the back room, he takes his lunch out of the safe, gets into another fight, in which he is almost beating his rival to death when the girl enters.

Charlot falls whimpering to the floor and is made much of. He returns to the counter and the episode of the clock begins.

A sinister figure enters, offering a clock in pawn. Charlot looks at it; then takes an auscultator and listens to its heartbeat; then taps it over crossed fingers for its pulmonary action; then taps it with a little hammer to see the quality, as with porcelain; then snaps his thumb on the bell. He takes an auger and bores a hole in it; then a can opener, and when he has pried the lid off he smells the contents and with a disparaging gesture makes the owner smell them, too. He then does dentistry on it, with forceps; then plumbing. Finally he screws a jeweler's magnifying glass into his eye and hammers what is left in the clock, shakes out the contents, measures the mainspring from the tip of his nose to arm's length, like cloth, squirts oil on the debris to keep it quiet, and, lifting the man's hat from his head, sweeps the whole mess into it and returns it with a sad shake of the head.

A pearl buyer has meanwhile come in and Charlot retraces his steps to the back room (carefully stepping over the buyer's hat) and begins to sweep. His broom becomes entangled with a piece of tape, which fights back and gets longer and longer. Suddenly Charlot begins to tightrope upon it, balancing with the broom, and making a quick turn, coming forward for applause. A final quarrel with the other assistant ensues. As they are swarming round the legs of the kitchen table, the boss comes in and Charlot flees, leaps into a trunk, and is hidden. As the others enter the room, the pearl buyer, who has stolen all the valuables, holds them up with a revolver. Charlot leaps from the trunk, fells the robber, and embraces the lovely maiden for a fade-out.

All of this takes about thirty minutes. I have put down nearly everything, for Chaplin is on the scene virtually all of the time. I am fairly certain that 90 percent of this film could not have been made, even badly, by anyone else. Analysis of *A Dog's Life* would give the same result: the arrival at the climax being a little more certain and the drama of the climax (the curtain scene—compared with the clock scene above) being more involved in the course of action.

The Kid (1921)

FRANCIS HACKETT

◆◇◆

The best motion pictures, I hear, are written with the scissors. The scissors, at any rate, have a great deal to do with the triumph of Charles Chaplin in (and with) *The Kid*. It is a movie stripped to its emotional essentials. The result is form, in which practically all American movies are just as much lacking as are our industrial architecture, display advertising, public cooking, and private conversation. In certain American institutions one does find form. Women's public meetings usually have it. The better sort of women's hats have it. So do certain kinds of house interiors and New England domestic architecture and those expositions of chamber music, baseball, and tennis which have never failed of appreciation here. But the movies are usually like the Sunday newspapers, Golden Oak furniture, Yonkers carpets, the snub-nosed and stub-toed Ford car. The moviemakers have simply wallowed in the license extended by American incompetence and indulgence, knowing that a people which puts its hotels in the noise-area and its hotel kitchens in the dust-area will be content to have its movies as loud and as insanitary as its life. It has remained for Charlie Chaplin to scout this indulgence, to adopt a standard absolutely and relatively high, and to be rewarded by the gratitude of millions. For millions of harassed and dissatisfied movie patrons are finding joy in the integrity of *The Kid*.

This integrity is to be enjoyed least of all in the anecdote itself. It is a silly enough story of a woman who is reunited with the child she deserted after a separation of some time and considerable space. A woman might conceivably abandon her baby in this fashion. There must be a score of abandoned babies for every few hundred abandoned women. But to fail to trace the baby at the time and yet to run into the growing child some years later—years gilded with success and yet yearning with heartache—is almost Shakespearean in its absurdity.

From The New Republic 26 *(March 30, 1921): 136–37. Reprinted by permission of Mrs. Signe Toksvig.*

Still, an excellent bean may be grown on the humblest of bean poles, and that is the case with *The Kid*. Chaplin knows that the story of his adopted waif is a joke between the experienced movie patron and himself. The merchantable maternal instinct and the surefire lost che-ild and the beautiful Lady Bountiful and the glad reunion—he glides over them with a touch like a light beam. What he has to play with is his own gorgeous predicament as the victim of a maternal problem. He has himself to present in the role of a Madonna. It is this pre-posterousness, with its possibilities of pathos and vulgarity, which he brings successfully through.

He does it as only a superb interpreter could. He realizes that when he, the authentic splay-footed, cane-twirling comedian, inherits the baby, he must steer his course clean away from farce in the direction of sentiment, but must keep enough comedy to correct the least hint of sentimentality. It gives him just the chance that his fine creative-ness demands. With a boldness that no other comedian could attempt, he exhibits himself feeding and providing for the baby. This boldness, which he pushes far enough to earn laughter and not so far as to ex-ploit it, he immediately banks up against his first exhibition of real feeling. And his exhibition of feeling is preserved from excess or un-reality by a resourcefulness in byplay which is beautifully right. He makes a contrast between The Kid's deportment, so sternly inculcated, and his own dilapidation, which never fails to give amusement; and he carries that dilapidation to extraordinary lengths. But just as he seems to have violated taste by projecting the dirty sole of his bare foot out of bed, his head is slipped through a hole in his bedspread—converting it into so comical a dressing gown that the very invasion of good taste is turned to grotesque account. This is only one of twenty tricks that he wins in his sly game with (or against) his audi-ence. He plays on his audience with an audacity that conquers prig and groundling in the same instant, and gives both of them a chance to be amused and moved.

Chaplin's relations to his audience may once have been deferential. Now he is an artist who uses his medium as he wills. When he opens the sewer trap and debates whether to slip the baby into it, he gains the credence which is only won by complete expressiveness. And his audience accepts his sincerity in this role of foster father with precisely the shade of amusement that he artfully conveys. To dominate pho-tography with a personality is in itself marvelous. It is all the more marvelous when one remembers that Chaplin is not a projection of the average but a variation, a sport. This violates in every detail the Philistinism which seems to be the motion-picture religion.

Without the Coogan boy it couldn't be done. It is dreadful to think of such a perfection as this child pushing out of his treble exquisiteness into something perhaps theatrical and overstimulated and unstable. But in his present manifestation, under the hand of Chaplin, he is as expressively and imaginatively natural as if he himself had Chaplin's genius. His eyes speak, and they say not only direct and eloquent things but things indirect, troubled, complicated. And not only do his eyes speak, but so do the turn of his head, his entrances and exits, his place on a lonely doorstep, or on a curb. No child that I have ever seen on the stage created so full a part before. Most of the children one sees are limited to one or two postures. They appear but do not represent. This "Kid" represents, and with a lovely mobile countenance, a countenance that is at once quite childlike and deep as an Italian masterpiece.

The dream of Heaven I thought highly amusing. What amused me was its limitedness, its meagerness. It was like a simple man's version of the Big Change, made up from the few properties with which a simple man would be likely to be acquainted. The lack of inventiveness seemed to me to be its best point. Others tell me that it was a failure of inventiveness. Mayhap. But after suffering the success of movie inventiveness so many times, with the whole apparatus of the factory employed to turn out some sort of slick statement or other, I rejoice over this bit of thin and faltering fantasy. And I venture to believe that it represents exactly what Chaplin intended. It was the simplified Heaven of that antic sprite whom Chaplin has created and whose inner whimsicality is here so amusingly indulged.

Chaplin's lightness of touch is shown not merely in the pictures, with the sporting elimination of unnecessary detail and the occasional note of mocking sophistication. It is shown technically in the admirable insistence that the pantomime must tell the story without any particular help from the desiccated medium of words. To read titles is to impede the flow of feeling rather than to aid it. It is to distract the pictorial mind. By cutting out as many titles as possible Charles Chaplin and his company keep close to the visual, and the visual in their case is frequently the beautiful, because of the effort that has been made to represent by hieroglyphic, to eliminate and simplify. Nothing could be better than the way *The Kid* is launched: the mother's plain clothing, her Salvation Army bonnet, her listless walk, and her short brooding in that open-air cathedral of broken humanity, the city park. The quickening of pace when she sees the wealthy motor, just before it is stolen (with her baby in it), tells everything that a world of newspaper-readers needs to know. And the discovery of the baby, its awkward removal, its abandonment in the meanest of lanes until it falls into the surprised hands of the little hobo—this is also sufficiently pointed by the expert action of the company Chaplin has wisely chosen. His wisdom, his sincerity, his integrity, all exhibited in this film, should go some way to revolutionize motion-picture production in this country. From an industry *The Kid* raises production to an art. An art it should be, in spite of the long-suffering public.

The Pilgrim (1923)
ROBERT E. SHERWOOD

◆◆

Charlie Chaplin has made comedies that may be rated above *The Pilgrim* in point of hilarity—and if you must have instances, I offer *Shoulder Arms*, *A Dog's Life* and *The Kid*—but there has been none in all his long list of comic triumphs that was so typically a Chaplin picture.

The Pilgrim was almost a dramatization of Chaplin himself—an exposition of his point of view, a recitation of his creed.

The fundamental trait in Chaplin's character is his sublime irreverence. He is the supreme gamin, strutting about in the mantle of genius and thumbing his nose at all institutions that suggest dignity, importance, and fat-headed pomposity. Nothing is sacred to him—except humanity; nothing is immune from the thrust of his satire or from the slam of his explosive slapstick.

Chaplin is a persistent kidder. The person who, on meeting him, dares to take him seriously, instantly becomes an attractive target for his sly raillery. In his time, Chaplin had kidded the most profound intellectual into believing that he is a deep thinker; he has kidded clergymen into believing that he is as spiritual as a nun; he has kidded radicals into believing that his life is devoted to the accomplishment of a world revolution; he has kidded members of the aristocracy into believing that he is one of them. And all the time, he has retained the identity of Charlie Chaplin; he has remained an agnostic, in the most inclusive sense of the word.

Thus, when Chaplin impersonated a convict who disguised himself in clerical garb, he approximated autobiography. He arrived in a

From The Best Moving Pictures of 1922–23, *edited by Robert E. Sherwood* (Boston: Small, Maynard & Co., 1923), pp. 59–62.

small Western town, and was accepted by the local congregation as the shepherd of its flock. He delivered a spectacular sermon on David and Goliath, concluding with a flood of oratory so dramatic that it moved a small boy to unseemly applause—in response to which Charlie took a number of breathless curtain calls.

During the collection, Charlie reached nervously for a cigarette, tapped it reflectively on his thumbnail, and was about to guide it to his lips when the horrified countenances of the choir reminded him that clergymen don't smoke in church.

This was all Chaplinesque in the extreme. It emphasized strongly his utter disregard for the conventional, his unquenchable drollery and his ability to bamboozle the straitlaced, kiddable gentry who believed that virtue is its own protection against ridicule.

In *The Kid,* Chaplin realized the beauty of childhood, and of the love which childhood inspires. His scenes with Jackie Coogan were rich with legitimate sentiment. There was nothing of heart interest or sob-squeezing hokum about it; it was genuine, honest, real. But in *The Pilgrim,* Chaplin sought to make atonement for his glorification of childhood as it was embodied in Jackie Coogan. Characteristically enough, he represented childhood in its most obnoxious form.

After the spectacular church service, the minister was invited to tea at the home of a parishioner. His fellow guests at this mild affair were a garrulous lady, her subdued husband, and their child—the most offensive infant in the history of the world.

The child's father, played in remarkably adroit fashion by Syd Chaplin, engaged in embarrassed conversation with the rector, while the dear little kiddie frolicked about over their laps, hitting them vigorously, poking at their eyes, plastering them with flypaper and deluging them with goldfish. Charlie Chaplin feebly resisted these advances, humbly suggesting to the mischievous little fellow that he "go play with momma." But it was all useless. The child continued to maul the helpless visitor—just as thousands of children have mauled thousands of innocent bystanders since the day when the first infant learned to pipe the words, "Do it again."

Chaplin terminated this incident in the most unexpected and yet the most logical manner. When the guests marched into the dining room to partake of the afternoon collation, the terrible child trotted obediently at the minister's heels, endeavoring to hamstring him. Chaplin turned on the brat and, obeying an impulse that had been surging within him throughout the ordeal, administered a painless but authoritative kick against the child's abdomen, and sent him hurtling across the room.

There are many, no doubt, who will decry this seemingly brutal behavior; but there are others who will murmur, devoutly, "God! How I've wanted to do that."

At the conclusion of *The Pilgrim*, Charlie reverted to the beatific mood of *The Kid*, by way of proving that there is something sacred, after all. The little minister had been exposed, and turned over to a sheriff for delivery at the jail whence he had come.

The sheriff was a kindly soul, with a sense of charitable leniency that is sadly misplaced in an official. He led Chaplin along until they came to the Mexican border.

"Do you see those flowers?" the sheriff inquired, pointing into neutral territory. "Go pick me some."

Charlie Chaplin dashed obediently across the border and the sheriff, smiling, rode off. But Charlie, a stern slave to duty, sprinted after him, waving the bunch of flowers. The sheriff promptly kicked him back across the border.

Here was an episode that was as eloquent, as impressive, as profound as Wordsworth's "Ode to Duty." It was also considerably more amusing.

I have dwelt heavily upon the significant aspects of *The Pilgrim* (it is always a temptation to soar into symbolism when considering a Chaplin picture), but the real meat of the piece was furnished when the terrible child slipped a derby hat over a plum pudding, and when the villain applied a lighted candle to that portion of Charlie Chaplin's anatomy which George Jean Nathan politely terms his "sit-spot."

Charlie Chaplin is a great artist, an inspired tragedian—and everything else that the intellectuals say he is—but there never can be any doubt of the fact that he is fundamentally a clown; and it is when he is being most broadly, vulgarly, crudely funny that he approaches true genius.

Perhaps the most hilariously humorous aspect of *The Pilgrim* was provided by the Pennsylvania censors, who barred the picture from that sacrosanct State because, said they, it made the ministry look ridiculous.

A number of interested observers have been waiting, since then, to hear that the Pennsylvania censors have suppressed several thousand clergymen on the same charge.

With the Bunk Left Out
CHARLES W. WOOD

◈◈

The "hero" got into a humiliating quarrel and then shot himself. The woman he had loved, and who had sinned so terribly, repented bitterly and devoted her life thereafter to works of charity. The villain remained the same gay old dog he had always been. When last seen, he had about forgotten the girl and was coming down the road in his touring car on his way, apparently, to new adventures in luxury. When last seen, *she* was going up the same road, on the back of a peasant's wagon with her feet hanging off, two of the youngsters whom she was taking care of sitting by her side.

This was on the moving-picture screen. It was the climax, and the first-night audience held its breath as the two vehicles approached. Never in all my theater-going have I ever seen a climax quite so dramatic. What happened was this. The chauffeur of the big touring car saw the wagon ahead and turned out for it, without slacking his speed. The peasants went on with their song, while the girl laughed and hugged the kids to keep them from falling off, not even turning an eye toward the occupants of the touring car. And the gay old dog didn't see her. They just passed each other, as vehicles do nowadays, and were soon out of sight.

I say I have never seen such a thrilling climax. It is my conviction that America has never seen a more important moving picture. It was Charlie Chaplin's first sortie into serious drama. He made that drama live by the simple method of making it simple. Other producers have achieved great successes through what they have put into their pictures. Charlie Chaplin has achieved the most phenomenal success of all through what he has left out.

I had the wonderful privilege of spending an afternoon in Mr. Chaplin's studio several months ago while *A Woman of Paris* was in the process of production. I wrote a story about it at the time. Charlie Chaplin's stuff is always good copy, I reflected, but this would be ex-

From Collier's 72 *(November 17, 1923): 31.*

ceptional. I had watched the world's most famous funny man at work
on a serious masterpiece. He had talked with me intimately and freely
about his aims and methods. He had completely unmasked. It was a
rare opportunity for me, but I couldn't find a magazine anywhere
that would print that story.

The editors all said they didn't know what I was talking about. And
they were right. My story was all full of words, and the story of Charlie
Chaplin cannot be told in words. Leaving out words is his specialty.
Simplicity. The elimination of the unnecessary. One cannot even judge
Charlie Chaplin by what he does. It is what he doesn't do that makes
him great.

Years had elapsed, for instance, between the tragic suicide of Jean
Miller and the day when Marie St. Clair went out with those kids and
caught the ride in that peasant's wagon. But any other moving-picture
director, it seems to me, would have insisted upon Marie's looking,
not as time and the cheerful companionship of children would make
her look, but as a woman ought in all film logic to look, considering
that she had been through such terrible experiences.

But Charlie Chaplin allowed time to have its way. He allowed it to
erase the marks of tragedy on Marie's face as time would naturally do.
Also Jean was dead, and Mr. Chaplin allowed him to stay dead. The
ordinary producer would have insisted upon revamping that suicide,
for it is not permitted in the movies for a woman to be happy unless
the hero is alive to attend the ceremony. If Charlie had only had Jean
almost kill himself and recover, he might have produced a regular picture. The least he could do, it would seem, would be to give Marie
a halo of saintly sadness. She might pass out apples to the kids; but she
ought in all conscience to heave sighs of repentance while she was
doing so, or gaze skyward with a serene and stony chill. But Charlie
Chaplin managed to have her do much less than that. He managed to
have her be just what a girl who is giving a bunch of kids a good time
would naturally be, in spite of the terrible happenings of a few years
before. He didn't produce a regular picture; but he made Marie a
regular fellow, both when she was going wrong and when she was
going right.

Mr. Chaplin likewise found it unnecessary to hang his villain, or to
get him pushed into a deep cavern just as he was about to execute
some hellish plot. He didn't even make the villain leer and proclaim
to all concerned, so that everybody above the intelligence of a heroine
might easily perceive it, that all his ways were vile. Charlie's villain
was so attractive, and had such good manners and good taste in addition to his wealth, that one could understand how a girl in Marie's
situation might conceivably fall for him. He had the edge on the true

lover in several respects, as the more successful sinners in real life are very apt to have.

But, on the other hand, Charlie didn't find it necessary to be morbid in order to be realistic. He didn't strive for the conventional happy ending; but he didn't find it imperative to wind everything up in impenetrable gloom. There was a happy ending—as happy as the ending of such a story could be expected to be—but it was the happiness that comes from the discovery of how to make one's life worth while. Charlie didn't seem to think it necessary to load vice down with any artificial handicaps in order that virtue might compete with it on even terms.

Incidentally, *A Woman of Paris* should teach a lesson to other producers which they should be quite willing to learn. It should show them how they can make a lot more money than they are making now. Mr. Chaplin spent a fortune producing this picture; but the expense incurred was mostly in the time he spent in developing the *drama,* not on building palaces to be photographed and razed. He was pioneering and felt his way most cautiously, and expensively. But he blazed a trail. He completely demolished a score of sacred traditions. It seems that other producers must get a much clearer vision than they have ever had before because of his seven months' work on *A Woman of Paris.*

No one but the biggest fool on earth could have performed this miracle. I say it in all reverence. In all ages only the very wisest could ever play the fool successfully. A few centuries ago, about the only person worth knowing was the court fool. That was in the days of absolute monarchy. In these days of democracy, when everybody is boss, things aren't so altogether different. Charlie Chaplin, for some years now, has been the Fool at the Court of King Demos. He could be just as sincerely funny as he cared to be. Only in the so-called "serious" pictures has stupidity been compulsory. Charlie has not been afraid of us. He has been full of impudence and daring and we have loved him for it. *A Woman of Paris,* then, is not only important in itself. It is additionally important because it is Charlie Chaplin's.

The public may not like the film as I liked it. It may not be at all ready to accept Mr. Chaplin's serious views of life. But, having seen it, there will be a lot of things left out of the American vision which have never been left out before. And much of that which will be left out will be seen to be bunk.

The Idea in *The Gold Rush:* A Study of Chaplin's Use of the Comic Technique of Pathos-Humor
TIMOTHY J. LYONS

◆◇◆

Originally Chaplin's technique in film was distinctive in its goal of opposite emotions: pathos and humor. He manipulated audiences to laugh or cry, whichever he deemed necessary. It is the intent of this article to investigate Chaplin's use of the idea in *The Gold Rush* (1925) and to offer some suggestions about the relationship of this idea to the comic technique of pathos-humor.

The emotion of *pathos* is a complex one, open to a number of interpretations. Confusion exists between three relatively similar feelings: *pity, pathos,* and *bathos.* Pity is a feeling of compassion or understanding accompanying a shared grief for the humanity in a situation. *Bathos,* however, is based on a sentimentalized and highly personal identification along with a compulsive desire to express sadness, regardless of the seriousness in a situation. Borrowing elements from both of these emotions is *pathos,* an identification with the humanity in a grieved situation.

Chaplin's use of emotion in his films relates directly to his underlying idea. Within this realm of ideas, Chaplin was fascinated by the macabre. Personal accounts by his friends showed this fascination by the tricks he played on people. From the incident of the Donner Party disaster during the Gold Rush to California, Chaplin constructed one of the funniest scenes in *The Gold Rush,* in which Charlie boils his shoe for Thanksgiving dinner. Such a bizarre incident bears significantly on the technique of pathos-humor. In this particular film, Chaplin pursued more strenuously the serious element which may be noted earlier in *The Kid* and which was to grow in strength in his later films. Indeed, this serious element in *The Gold Rush* has moments "close to cruelty and grief." [1] At one moment in the film there is empathy with two men starving; at the next moment there is delight with Big Jim's cannibalistic vision of Charlie as a chicken. So skillfully has Chaplin accomplished his duality in this film, that Peter Cotes sees *The Gold Rush* as "filled with a rich humanity that strips him entirely of his earlier fantasy, his poetry, his almost mythological presentation" to become "the most perfect balance yet achieved by this tightrope walker, expert in treading delicately on the verge of the opposite emotions." [2]

Chaplin himself chronicled the idea formulation for *The Gold Rush*:

I was now free to make my first comedy for United Artists and anxious to top the success of *The Kid*. For weeks I strove, thought, and brooded, trying to get an idea. I kept saying to myself: "This next film must be an epic! The greatest!" But nothing would come. Then one Sunday morning, while spending the weekend at the Fairbanks', I sat with Douglas after breakfast, looking at stereoscopic views. Some were of Alaska and the Klondike; one a view of the Chilkoot Pass, with a long line of prospectors climbing up over its frozen mountain, with a caption printed on the back describing the trials and hardships endured in surmounting it. This was a wonderful theme, I thought, enough to stimulate my imagination. Immediately ideas and comedy business began to develop and, although I had no story, the image of one began to grow.

In the creation of comedy, it is paradoxical that tragedy stimulates the spirit of ridicule, because ridicule, I suppose, is an attitude of defiance: we must laugh in the face of our helplessness against the forces of nature—or go insane. I read a book about the Donner Party, who on the way to California missed the route and were snowbound in the Sierra Nevada mountains. Out of 160 pioneers only 18 survived, most of [the casualties] dying of hunger and cold. Some resorted to cannibalism, eating their dead, others roasted their moccasins to relieve their hunger. Out of this harrowing tragedy I conceived one of our funniest scenes. In dire hunger I boil my shoe and eat it, picking the nails as though they were bones of a delicious capon, and eating the shoelaces as though they were

[1] Vsevolod Meyerhold, "Chaplin and Chaplinism," *Tulane Drama Review*, 11 (Fall 1966), 190.
[2] Peter Cotes and Thelma Niklaus, *The Little Fellow* (New York: Citadel Press, 1965), p. 120.

spaghetti. In this delirium of hunger, my partner is convinced I am a chicken and wants to eat me.[3]

This above quote suggests the following points to be covered: (1) Chaplin's desire to make "an epic! The greatest!" (2) the importance of the Donner Party to this epic concern; (3) the influence of the Donner Party on Chaplin's spirit of ridicule; and (4) the implication of man's inhumanity to man as a recurrent theme with Chaplin.

I. THE EPIC NATURE

With the completion of *The Pilgrim* in 1922, Chaplin had fulfilled his contract with First National Films. The United Artists Corporation, of which Chaplin was a founding member, had already been functioning for three years when Chaplin began the serious film *A Woman of Paris*. The disappointing box-office return from this film probably had a great effect on Chaplin's decision to do a comedy. At the same time, Chaplin had tasted critical praise for his direction of *A Woman of Paris* and was anxious to strengthen his directing reputation in an epic production.

Many strong figures had preceded him in applying epic form to film. D. W. Griffith had made the spectaculars *Birth of a Nation* (1915), *Intolerance* (1916), *Way Down East* (1920), and *Orphans of the Storm* (1921), the latter two under the banner of United Artists. Robert Flaherty had produced *Nanook of the North* (1922), perhaps the first film to explore the possibilities of full-length documentary—*and* with a snow-covered location. Cecil B. DeMille had also startled the movie-going public with the epic *Ten Commandments* (1923). In comedy, Harold Lloyd had utilized danger on a grand scale in *Safety Last* (1923)—a highlight of the film showing Harold hanging precariously from a clock tower high above the city streets. Perhaps it can be suggested that the picturemakers mentioned above influenced Chaplin greatly in his decision to make an epic film with a universal message accompanied by spectacular action—but the comparison can be carried only this far.

This epic concern appears contributary to the development of the pathos-humor technique. Previous Chaplin films accented the character of the tramp; comic situations grew from battles with props such as the deck chair in *A Day's Pleasure,* the wall-bed in *One A.M.,* and the clock in *The Pawnshop.* Comic situations also found Charlie bat-

[3] Charles Chaplin, *My Autobiography* (New York: Simon and Schuster, 1964), pp. 303–5.

tling authority figures such as policemen. The environment of these earlier films did not take a predominant part in the comedy; the accent was on Charlie himself. This accentuation was a limiting emotional factor, since the majority of these films found the tramp in lower-class surroundings, often the slums like those of *The Kid.* Hence, the tramp became associated with the lower classes and as such limited audience empathy. The real pathos began to blend with the humor when the general audience could identify with Charlie and did not need the experience of the particular environment to accomplish this identification. By moving the environment from the city streets to the snow-covered plains, Chaplin was able to accomplish this audience identification to a greater degree by expanding the settings, both in number and variety. The epic setting of *The Gold Rush* dominates well over half the scenes in the film.

Chaplin utilized Nature as a predominant part in the film. The opening scenes showed the vast expanses of snow which men faced in their struggle to overcome the North. Blizzards and storms raged throughout the film causing a number of events to occur: (1) Charlie sought refuge in Black Larsen's cabin; (2) Big Jim was blown into the cabin; and (3) the cabin was blown to the edge of a cliff. In a resolution scene, Black Larsen was killed when the cliff on which he was standing avalanched to the valley below. The power of Nature was seen in these scenes as one of the major forces opposing the gold-rush prospectors.

But the force of Nature also provided humor in the scenes where the three men were blown in and out of the cabin, where Charlie watched the force of the wind push in on the cabin wall, where Charlie shovelled snow to earn money for his dinner party, and when the cabin rocked on the cliff's edge.

In spite of these epic forces and the fear and apprehension evoked by them, the audience recognized that Charlie was not in serious danger; they could laugh at these moments, but their laughter was based partly on the pathetic elements involved. However, the technique used by Chaplin to arouse such laughter had already begun to shift with this film. *The Gold Rush* was not wholly comic; Chaplin himself subtitled it *A Dramatic Comedy.*[4]

II. The Donner Party: Its Importance to the Epic Nature

When asked about the Donner Party and its influence on Chaplin's film, Chaplin's veteran cameraman, Roland H. Totheroh replied:

[4] Theodore Huff, *Charlie Chaplin* (New York: Pyramid, 1964), p. 154.

That really gave him the idea to go ahead and make *The Gold Rush*. He had read the book *The Donner Party*; in fact, that's where our location was, up there in Truckee on the summit, near the Donner Party statue. All of that scene with Mack Swain and the chicken . . . was based on the Donner Party cannibalism.[5]

The gold-rush period of this nation was filled with tragedies of pioneers, sudden success, and equally sudden failure. By basing this film on such subject matter, Chaplin added to the potentiality for pathos.

Chaplin stated in his autobiography that he had "read a book about the Donner Party." A letter from George R. Stewart, noted California historian and expert on the Donner Party chronicles, suggests that "Chaplin probably read McGlashan's book, but the figures in the autobiography are all wrong." [6] In 1924, few books were available concerning the Donner Party; however, one particular book, C. F. McGlashan's *History of the Donner Party*, received a new printing in 1922 and was on bookshop shelves.[7] McGlashan's account seems to relate very significantly to the episodes of *The Gold Rush;* moreover, McGlashan stresses the epic quality of the Donner Party disaster, showing the helplessness against the mighty forces of nature. In both the epic quality and the macabre situation *The Gold Rush* shows an affinity to McGlashan.

Five main points are similar to episodes in the chronicle, two of which (location and time) are related to the epic portrait, and three (cannibalism, cabin, and the bear) to Chaplin's use of ridicule of tragic situations.

The Donner Party was snowbound just outside of what is now Truckee, California, near Donner Lake and the famous pass named after the pioneering group. Chaplin spent many months near Truckee shooting footage, carving the mock Chilkoot Pass out of the nearby mountainside.[8] Perhaps this removal to the actual scene of the tragedy

---

[5] From an interview with Roland H. Totheroh at the Motion Picture Country House, Woodland Hills, California, on 8 April 1967.

[6] From a letter dated 3 February 1967 in response to inquiry by this writer.

[7] Charles Fayette McGlashan, *History of the Donner Party* (San Francisco: A. Carlisle and Co.. 1922). The book was originally published in 1879, thirty-two years following the Donner Party tragedy. Historical records and eyewitness accounts were used as supporting material in the book. Chaplin's mistake on the actual number of pioneers was due probably to faulty recollection (his autobiography being written forty years after the reading of the book), since all the available books on the subject had essentially the same historical information; only the treatment in these books varied.

[8] Lita Grey Chaplin, *My Life With Chaplin* (New York: Bernard Geis Associates, 1966), pp. 58–70.

can be seen as a further attempt by Chaplin to reach this epic quality in his film. In this removal, Chaplin also managed to interlock humor with the pathos of this tragic location.

The time of the year in which the Donner Party suffered their tragedy was from the spring of 1846 through the winter of 1847. McGlashan follows this period chronologically with verified newspaper and eyewitness accounts. Three holidays are mentioned in the book: Thanksgiving, Christmas, and New Year's Day; likewise, *The Gold Rush* utilizes activities on Thanksgiving and New Year's. "On New Year's morning they ate their moccasins and the strings of their snowshoes," wrote McGlashan.[9] Such a scene occurs in the film, but as a Thanksgiving feast. Charlie attempts to appease the starving Big Jim and his own stomach as well by boiling the only appetizing thing in sight: Charlie's right shoe. The scene is comical in portrayal, but the underlying pathos of the situation is heavy. New Year's Eve in *The Gold Rush* finds Charlie waiting anxiously for his invited guests to arrive for dinner: he waits in vain since Georgia and the dance-hall girls have forgotten him. The nature of Thanksgiving and New Year's Day as holidays is one of reflection for the American public. At least in theory, the days represent a nostalgic recalling of past events and a reinforced hope for the future. Whether conscious or not, the feast of boiled shoe for Thanksgiving dinner touched the hearts of an audience; the comedy was there, of course, but a deeper identification with the situation occurred. When Charlie was forced to spend the festive New Year's Eve standing out in the cold, watching the celebration through the dance-hall window, this incident struck at the pathos of the entire situation. Had this happened on any other evening, besides New Year's Eve, perhaps the pathos would not have been as great.

III. The Donner Party: Its Importance to the Spirit of Ridicule

In location and time, *The Gold Rush* follows McGlashan's report closely. At the same time, both aspects relate significantly to the epic quality desired by Chaplin. The ridicule of the location and of the time is also present. This ridicule, combined with the seriousness of the situation, is directly applicable to the humor and pathos in technique.

The fascination with the macabre and the subsequent ridicule of the tragic is seen in the examples of cannibalism, the cabin, and the bear. The cannibalism of the Donner Party was the major incident

---

[9] McGlashan, p. 86.

placing the group in history. Many pioneers had braved the Rockies and the Sierra Nevada Mountains but received much less coverage than did the Donner Party. Out of ninety pioneers, only forty-eight survived the hardships.[10] This point of cannibalism was used comically by Chaplin in the scene where Big Jim sees Charlie as a chicken and wants to eat him. The comedy in the scene is high; yet here were two men on the verge of starvation, one contemplating cannibalism, and the other "hopping" to avoid it. Out of this harrowing incident, the comedy evolved through ridicule. McGlashan reported the various incidents of cannibalism periodically throughout his book, in the most vivid detail. After a relief party reached the Donner group, McGlashan reports, "So hungry were the poor people that some of them ate the strings of the snowshoes which the relief company had brought along." [11] In the boiled-shoe-eating scene, Charlie eats his shoestrings as though they were spaghetti; the result is comedy, but again an underscoring of deep pathos in the idea of death from starvation.

Much of the action in *The Gold Rush* occurs in the cabin occupied by Black Larsen. Charlie and Big Jim become the uninvited guests and remain as Larsen departs in search of food. Later in the film the twosome returns to the cabin to spend the night, waking to find themselves teetering precariously on the edge of a cliff, the cabin being suspended only by a rope. The cabin itself was constructed in a makeshift manner, utilizing two doorways, a window, and a back shed. A similar cabin is reported by McGlashan as the secene of one of the original incidents of cannibalism:

> Foster, Montgomery, and Schallenberger built the cabin. Two days were spent in its construction. It was built of pine saplings, and roofed of pine brush and rawhides. It was twelve by fourteen feet, and seven or eight feet high, with a chimney in one end, built "western style." One opening, through which light, air, and the occupants passed, served as a window and door. . . . The Breen family moved into the Schallenberger cabin. Against the west side of this cabin, Keseberg built a sort of half shed, into which he and his family entered.[12]

The cabin of *The Gold Rush* resembled greatly the cabin reported above. The very makeshift style of construction emphasized the lack of preparation by the Donner Party. This lack of preparation, and Chaplin's subsequent ridicule of the fact, also served to emphasize the opening lines of the narrative in the film:

[10] McGlashan, "Introduction," p. vi.
[11] McGlashan, p. 135.
[12] McGlashan, pp. 61–62.

During the great Gold Rush to Alaska, men in thousands came from all parts of the world. Many of them were ignorant of the hardships before them, the intense cold, the lack of food, and a journey through regions of ice and snow was the problem that awaited them.[13]

A bear is seen twice in *The Gold Rush* and serves as a dangerous threat in each case. In the opening scene of the film, Charlie walks along a narrow cliff followed by a large grizzly bear. The tramp is oblivious to the bear's presence, and when Charlie does turn around, the bear has just entered a nearby cave and disappeared from sight. A similar incident is reported by McGlashan:

> Mr. Clark at once followed [the bear], tracking it up the mountain side to a cliff of rocks, and losing the trail at the mouth of a small dark cave. . . . Judging from the tracks, and from the size of the cub he had seen, Mr. Clark concluded that it was possible he might be able to enter the cave and kill the cub in a hand-to-hand fight.[14]

A bear also appears after Charlie and Big Jim have struggled for possession of the rifle. Big Jim, having just revived from the hallucination of Charlie as a chicken, pulls a blanket over Charlie's head and rushes for the gun. A huge grizzly enters from the shed and frightens Jim away. Charlie grabs the bear's back leg and continues the struggle, assuming the bear to be Jim. When the blanket falls, Charlie runs from the bear, which exits nonchalantly through the front door. When Jim reenters, Charlie grabs the rifle, shoots the bear, and sends Jim out to retrieve their feast.

In McGlashan's book, a grizzly bear served as appetizing relief for the starving group of people. Their supplies depleted, the Donner Party feasted at one point when a large grizzly was killed:

> I was startled by a snuffling, growling noise, and looking up, I saw a large grizzly bear only a few feet away. I knew I was too weak to attempt to escape, and so remained where I sat, expecting every moment he would devour me. Suddenly there was the report of a gun and the bear fell dead.[15]

The great danger of this beast was offset by the relief its carcass provided to the starving men. At this point, Chaplin managed this

---

[13] Timothy J. Lyons, comp., *"The Gold Rush: A Screenplay," Cinema* (Beverly Hills) 4 (Summer 1968): 18.

[14] McGlashan, p. 167.

[15] McGlashan, p. 216.

"ridicule" of overpowering forces by showing the serious threat of the
bear and the help it eventually provided.

Other minor incidents are reported by McGlashan which might be
connected with some of the incidents in *The Gold Rush* in epic quality, macabre appearance, and subsequent ridicule of the tragic situation by Chaplin in the film. Pioneers buried in snowdrifts and ava-
lanches, signposts announcing the locations of graves, and claim-
jumpers and squatters usurping land granted to the Donners—all are
found in this report and can be seen in slightly altered fashion in
The Gold Rush. The epic presentation of McGlashan's account,
coupled with the ridicule by Chaplin and his fascination with the
macabre and the tragic, all led to significant contributions to the
pathos-humor technique in the film.

IV. Man's Inhumanity to Man

One of the major themes of *The Gold Rush*—and indeed of many
Chaplin films—is that of man's inhumanity to man. The underdog
trampled by the money-grabbers: this was the presentation in the
films.

Specific instances in this film reflect this view. In the opening scene,
a prospector stumbles while climbing up the narrow pass, and the line
of men pass him by, not one stopping to lend him aid. Charlie and
Big Jim are certainly not welcomed into Black Larsen's cabin, although a storm was raging outside. In the dance hall, Charlie suffers
the taunts and rejections from the crowd. When the tramp finally has
made his fortune, the multimillionaire is besieged by well-wishers, the
press, and the steamship's crew.

Chaplin shows how those with no worldly possessions are recognized only when they rise in wealth. This theme is underlying
throughout the film, yet is overshadowed mostly by the comedy in the
situations. Chaplin himself recognized the problem of having a girl
fall in love with the tramp:

> But logically it was difficult to get a beautiful girl interested in
> the tramp. This has always been a problem in my films. In *The
> Gold Rush* the girl's interest in the tramp started by her playing
> a joke on him, which later moves her to pity, which he misinter-
> prets as love.[16]

Yet when the tramp finally wins his fortune, the roles are reversed:
now Georgia needs him. In the middle of the film, we see Charlie's

[16] Chaplin, p. 210.

infatuation with Georgia; in a sense, he needs her. After he has made his fortune, he meets Georgia on the ship. She is traveling to America with third-class accommodations and little hope for a new kind of life; in a sense, she now needs Charlie. And for the first time in a Chaplin film, the tramp wins the girl. The mistreatment which he has undergone has been worthwhile.[17]

Basic to Chaplin's treatment of epic focus, of ridicule, and of man's inhumanity was the particular quality of Chaplin's comic art, which stressed the rebounding qualities of the tramp. This seems clearly associated with the combination of pathos and humor. If the episodes of mistreatment occurred to a down-and-out prospector unable to rebound, the comedy would be lost. But Charlie can and does spring back. He remains in Larsen's cabin and makes the best of his hunger by eating the candle in a nearby lantern; later, he boils his own shoe. He brushes himself off after a ridiculous bout with a dog, whose leash Charlie used as a belt, and joins the laughter of the crowd. After banging his hand against a post in the dance hall, a clock falls and hits Charlie's opponent; when Charlie manages to wrench his hat free from his head and can again see clearly, he assumes it was his powerful punch that floored Jack Cameron. Like the conquering hero, he strides out of the dance hall.

An element predominant in Chaplin's comedy is this rebounding aspect. Chaplin arouses laughter partly because of the audience's admiration for him. The audience does not feel, as Al Capp wrongly suggests,[18] that they are superior to him; indeed, Charlie reacts admirably to the situation and the audiences applaud his resourcefulness. When Charlie is faced with a situation, perhaps the audience feels superior to him in that they themselves would not have allowed such a situation to occur. This superiority, however, breaks down when the audience witnesses Charlie's resourcefulness in the situation. He retains his dignity in the face of ridicule; no matter what happens to Charlie, he is still a self-sufficient human being.

The comedy here lies in the fact that derision and ridicule themselves work only when the character undergoing this ridicule is capable of recovering from such an attack or is insensitive to such mistreatment. For a policeman to beat a sickly alcoholic who was sleeping in the park is cruelty; yet for a hobo to ask for another kick because it feels so good when the officer stops—this is comedy. In *The Gold*

---

[17] Chaplin might be making an ironic comment with the ending of *The Gold Rush*: As he and Georgia embrace, the camera man from the press shouts, "Oh, you've spoilt the picture!" Could this have been the filmmaker's attempt to forestall the critics' objections?

[18] Al Capp, "The Comedy of Charlie Chaplin," *Atlantic Monthly*, 185 (February 1950): 25–29.

Rush Charlie also remains insensitive to mistreatment or danger. In the opening scene when Charlie is being followed closely by a huge grizzly, he is unaware of the danger present; the audience laughs at his ignorance. The repeated taunts of Jack Cameron to Charlie do not affect the tramp; he is insensitive to such inhumanity. Despite the serious theme of man's inhumanity to man, Chaplin rises above the situation comically by the means suggested above.

The idea of this film can be seen as significant in terms of the comic technique of pathos-humor. Chaplin felt the need to make an epic film, which in turn led to a perfection in his comedy by moving the tramp from the streets, battling society and environment, to struggle against Nature and her forces. With the decision to base his story on the incidents of the Donner Party, Chaplin concentrated on what he called "the spirit of ridicule" as an attitude toward tragedy. From the tragic and macabre incidents suggested by McGlashan's chronicle, Chaplin managed to render a humorous presentation; at the same time, the underlying pathos of the situation being shown blended with the humorous presentation.

The theme of man's inhumanity to man, especially in the search for possession, has been seen as an undercurrent in Chaplin's comedies. This aspect led to the fact that derision and ridicule themselves do not necessarily produce a comedy. The comedy in a Chaplin film arises from the tramp's ability to rebound under the most dire of circumstances or to remain insensitive to any attack. The fact that Charlie was subjected to mistreatment does not produce the comedy; the dignified reaction and the chance victories over this mistreatment are the essential elements of Chaplin's comedy. As with the seriousness of the Donner Party, the derision and ridicule also act as undercurrents producing pathos.

A Comparison of *The Gold Rush* and *The General*
GERALD MAST

◆◆◆

Only Buster Keaton could rival Chaplin in his insight into human relationships, into the conflict between the individual man and the immense social machinery that surrounds him; only Keaton could rival Chaplin in making his insight both funny and serious at the same time. On the one hand, the Keaton canon as a whole is thinner, less consistent than the Chaplin canon; the character he fashioned, with his deadpan, blank reaction to the chaos that inevitably and inadvertently blooms around him, lacks the range, the compassionate yearnings, the pitiable disappointments of Chaplin's tramp. On the other hand, Keaton fashioned a single film, *The General,* that is possibly more even, more unified, and more complex in both conception and execution than any individual Chaplin film.

The key difference between Keaton and Chaplin is that Charlie longs to better himself, to accomplish grand things, whereas Keaton merely desires to go about his business. If he fails to reach his modest goal it is not because of his own incompetence or ineptitude but because of the staggeringly huge obstacles the environment throws in his path to keep him from getting there. Objects inevitably play a role in Keaton films, but unlike the objects in a Chaplin film, which are small, manageable, which Charlie can hold in his hand, or lie in, or sit on, the objects in a Keaton film are immense machines which dwarf the little man. Keaton plays against huge things—an ocean liner which he must navigate by himself, a locomotive, a steamboat. When he runs into trouble with men, it is never with a single figure (an Eric Campbell); he runs into rivers of antagonists, into armies of opponents—a whole tribe of jungle savages, the entire Union and Confederate armies. Like Charlie, Buster has troubles with cops, but never

From Cinema Journal *9 (Spring 1970): 24–30. This essay is included in* A Short History of the Movies *by Gerald Mast (New York: Pegasus). Reprinted by permission of Pegasus, A Division of Western Publishing.*

with one or a few cops; Buster (in *Cops,* in *Daydreams*) runs into the entire police force. Given the size and complexity of his problems, Buster can take no sensible or meaningful action, despite his most sensible efforts. The perfect metaphor for the Keaton man is in the short film, *Daydreams,* in which Buster, to avoid the police force, has taken refuge in the paddle wheel of a ferryboat. The wheel begins turning; Buster begins walking. And walking. And walking. He behaves as sensibly as a man can on a treadmill that he cannot control, but how sensible can life on a treadmill ever be?

Chaplin and Keaton are the two poles of silent comics. Chaplin's great strength is his development of character and the exhausting of a particular comic and social situation; Keaton's strength is the tightness of his narrative structures and his contrast between the numbers one and infinity. Chaplin is sentimental; his gentle, smiling women become idols to be revered. Keaton is not sentimental; he stuffs his females into bags and hauls them around like sacks of potatoes; he satirizes their finicky incompetence and even raises his fist to the silly lady in *The General* who feeds their racing locomotive only the teensiest shavings of wood. It was especially appropriate and touching to see the two opposites, Chaplin and Keaton, united in *Limelight* (1952), both playing great clowns who were losing their audiences and their touch.

No two films more clearly reveal the contrasting strengths and interests of the two clowns than *The Gold Rush* and *The General,* both of which were released in the same year, 1925. Like the short comedies, *The Gold Rush* is an episodic series of highly developed, individual situations. The mortar that keeps these bricks together is a mixture of the film's locale (the white, frozen wastes), the strivings and disappointments of Charlie, and the particular thematic view the film takes of those strivings (the quest for gold and for love, those two familiar goals, in an icy cannibalistic jungle). All the Chaplin features, including those he made with synchronized sound, would share this common episodic structure. *The Gold Rush* also benefits from the circular pattern of the sequence of episodes: Prologue (the journey to Alaska), the Cabin, the Dance Hall, New Year's Eve, the Dance Hall, the Cabin, Epilogue (the journey home).

The individual sequences of *The Gold Rush* are rich both in Chaplin's comic ingenuity and in his ability to render the pathos of the tramp's disappointment, his cruel rejection by the woman he loves. Several of the comic sequences have become justifiably famous. In the first cabin scene a hungry Charlie cooks his shoe, carves it like a prime rib of beef, salts it to taste, and then eats it like a gourmet, twirling the shoelaces around his fork like spaghetti, sucking the nails in the soles like chicken bones, offering his friend one of the nails as a wishbone. This is the Chaplin who treats one kind of object (a shoe) as if it were another kind of object (a feast), the same minute observation he used in dissecting the clock in *The Pawnshop*. In the dance hall, Charlie hastily ties a rope around his middle to keep his sagging trousers up. He does not know that the other end of the rope is attached to a dog, who then trots around the dance floor following his dancing master. Charlie, however, must follow the leader when the dog takes off after a cat. But the comic business is matched by the pathos that Charlie can generate, often itself growing out of comic business.

Charlie's saddest moment is when Georgia, the woman he loves, whose picture and flower he preserves beneath his pillow, callously stands him up on New Year's Eve. When Charlie realizes that it is midnight and that she is not coming, he opens his door and listens to the happy townspeople singing "Auld Lang Syne." The film cuts back and forth between Charlie, the outsider, standing silently and alone in a doorway, and the throng of revelers in the dance hall, clasping hands in a large circle and singing exuberantly together. But this pathetic moment would have been impossible without the previous comic one in which Charlie falls asleep and dreams he is entertaining Georgia with his "Oceana Roll." Charlie's joy, his naive sincerity, his charm, his gentleness all show on his face as he coyly makes the two rolls kick, step, and twirl over the table on the ends of two forks. The happiness of the comic dream sequence creates the pathos of the subsequently painful reality.

If the reality proves painful for Charlie it is because the lust for gold makes it so. The film's theme is its consistent indictment of what the pursuit of the material does to the human animal; as in *Greed*, it makes him an inhuman animal. Charlie the least materialistic of men, has come to the most materialistic of places—a place where life is hard, dangerous, brutal, uncomfortable and unkind. Unlike the life of Nanook (might Chaplin have been influenced by Flaherty?) in which hardness becomes a virtue in itself, the men who have rushed for gold want to endure hardship temporarily, just long enough to snatch up enough nuggets to go home and live easy. The quest for gold perverts all human relationships in the film. It creates a Black Larsen who casually murders and purposely fails to help his starving fellows. It creates a Jack, Georgia's handsome boyfriend, who treats his fellow men and women like furniture. Just as Charlie's genuine compassion reveals the emptiness of Jack's protestations of love, Chaplin's film technique makes an unsympathetic villain out of the conventional Hollywood leading man. The rush toward gold perverts both love and friendship. Georgia herself, though Charlie perceives her inner beauty, has become hardened and callous from her strictly cash relationships with people in the isolated dance hall. And Charlie's friend, Big Jim McKay, is one of those fairweather friends whose feelings are the functions of expediency. When Big Jim gets hungry he literally tries to eat Charlie; although Jim's seeing his buddy as a big chicken is comic, the implied cannibalism of the sequence is not. Later, Big Jim needs Charlie to direct him to his claim; once again Charlie becomes friend because he is needed. But when Jim and Charlie get stuck in the cabin that teeters precariously off a cliff, the two men turn into dogs again, each trying to scramble out of the cabin by himself, stepping on each other to do so.

Whereas *The Gold Rush* combines a thematic unity with the episodic structure of exhausting the individual situations, the thematic coherency of *The General* is itself the product of the film's tight narrative unity. *The General* is a comic epic in film form. Like every comic epic, *The General* is the story of a journey, of the road (albeit a railroad). As in every comic epic, the protagonist suffers a series of hardships and dangerous adventures before achieving the rewards and comforts of returning home. The protagonist's opponents are both man and nature, particularly those two epic natural enemies, fire and water. There is a comic insufficiency in the protagonist and a disproportion between his powers and the task he is asked to accomplish; but like every protagonist in the comic epic, Buster triumphs despite his insufficiencies. Everything in the Chaplin film, every gag, every piece of business, every thematic contrast, is subordinate to the delineation of the lonely tramp's character and the qualities that make him both lonely and superior to the men who have betrayed their humanity to keep from being lonely. Everything in *The General*, every gag, every piece of business, is subordinate to driving the film's narrative, its story of Johnny Gray's trying to save his three loves—his girl, his country, and, most important of all, his locomotive. *The Gold Rush* is a comedy of character, *The General* a comedy of narrative.

The great question that *The General* poses in the course of its narrative is how to perform heroic action in a universe that is not heroic. Buster, with his typical deadpan expression merely tries to go about his business while the world around him goes mad. A metaphor for the feeling of the whole film is the shot in which Buster is so busy chopping wood to feed his engine that he fails to notice that the train is racing past row after row of blue uniforms marching in the contrary direction. Johnny Gray has inadvertently propelled himself behind the enemy's lines. Johnny Gray simply wants to run his train; unfortunately, the Union army wants to steal that train and then use it to destroy his fellow Confederates. In the course of merely trying to save the train, Johnny rescues his lady love and wins a terrific victory for the South, quite by accident.

That heroism becomes an accident in *The General* is at the center of its moral thrust. It is an accident that the cannon, aimed squarely at Johnny, does not go off until the train rounds a curve, discharging its huge ball at the enemy instead of at the protagonist. It is an accident that Buster's train comes to a rail switch just in time to help it detour the pursuing Union train. Whereas wealth, material success, is accidental in *The Gold Rush* (and an accident not worth waiting for), heroism and successful military strategy are accidental in *The General*. And just as Charlie's character exposes the folly of the accidents of wealth, Buster's character exposes the folly of the accidents of heroism. For how less heroic, how less aspiring, less grand can a man be than little Buster? Buster merely uses his shrewd common sense against impossible odds, and he is lucky to get away with it.

The denigration of the heroic is as constant an element of *The General's* narrative as the denigration of gold in the sequences of *The Gold Rush*. The plot is triggered by Johnny Gray's rejection by the Confederate Army. He fears he has been found wanting, but the Confederacy needs him vitally at home, running his locomotive. Nevertheless, his girl and her family ostracize Johnny as an unheroic coward, a shirker, and the rest of the film demonstrates what heroism really is and what it is really worth. Johnny uses the most pragmatic, least heroic of tools for defeating the Northern Army—boxes of freight, pieces of wood from a fence, the locomotive's kerosene lantern. Hardheadedness, not gallantry, wins the day. The gallant and romantic receive explicit burlesque in the film's final sequence, the battle, in which victory comes as a combination of stupidity and chance. The Northern general, certain that the bridge Johnny earlier set afire is still strong enough to support his supply train, orders it across. The general is wrong; the train and bridge topple magnificently into the river below.

In the pitch of battle Johnny sees the Confederate standard about to fall to the ground. He hastily climbs to what he thinks is a hilltop in a gallant gesture to support the falling flag (a parody of Griffith?), only to discover the embarrassment of feeling the hilltop move. The hilltop is really a disgruntled soldier's back. When Johnny Gray solemnly inducted into the Confederate Army for his bravery, and the sequence uses all the formal rigamarole of military honor, Buster heroically draws his sword only to see the blade fall off, leaving a stubby handle in his upstretched arm. When the Northern officer surrenders to the South according to all the articles and procedures of war, Johnny Gray accidentally fires his pistol, disrupting the dignified formality of the ceremony. Even the film's ending burlesques the conventions of heroism, war, and romance. Johnny wraps his arms

around his girl for the final clinch; since he is now an officer, all
soldiers must salute him and he must salute in return. In the midst
of his embrace, the entire battalion troops past him. After interrupt-
ing his embrace for a while, he, in his pragmatic manner, devises a
better method. He continues saluting perfunctorily and mechanically,
never taking his lips or his eyes away from hers.

Such antiheroism is common to all Keaton films; he is always the
sensible little guy who inadvertently runs up against senseless objects
that dwarf him. The element that distinguishes *The General* is that
the senseless object, the huge infernal machine of this film, is war. Men
themselves have been transformed into a machine (an army), and the
business of this machine is murder and destruction. This antiheroic
comic epic must necessarily become an antiwar story too, for the military heroism that *The General* consistently debunks is the Circe that
turns men into murdering and destructive swine. Buster never is
hypnotized, and his film makes sure we keep our eyes open too.

There is absolutely nothing sentimental in the world of *The General*. As soon as Johnny Gray gets a bit sad, Keaton immediately slams
him with a joke to rip the pathos off him. The film is as shrewd, as
caustic, as hard-edged as Johnny Gray himself. His girl, a typical
figure of sentiment and romance, is degraded into an incompetent and
feeble representative of romantic notions; Johnny Gray ultimately
must fight her as well as the pursuing army. There is no place in the
world of *The General* for sentiment, for the same reason that there
is no place for heroism. Romance and heroism are twins, and *The
General* wages war on the whole family. Unlike the Chaplin films,
there are no flowers, no roses, in *The General*. As soon as you admit a
rose, you must also admit a gun to fight for it. True, the character Buster plays, Johnny Gray, is a Southerner, a seeming romantic choice.
But Buster chose to play a rebel because the South lost the war,
because the South was the little-guy underdog (like Buster), and because the South was the romantically blindest about fighting the war
in the first place. Though Johnny plays a Southerner the film is im-
partial; ultimately Johnny must sneak his train (even its name is a
military one) past both the Union and the Confederate lines. Despite
the film's comic conclusion and inventive gags, *The General*, with its
mixture of burlesque and grimness (many men die in this film), is the
spiritual ancestor of that recent mixture of laughs and war horrors,
Doctor Strangelove.

The ultimate proof of the power of *The Gold Rush* and *The General*
is that they need not be referred to as great silent films; they are merely
great films. They require no qualification of any kind (unlike even Griffith's greatest work). For both of them silence was not a limitation but a

virtue. It is inconceivable that the two films could have been any better
with sound; in fact, by removing our complete concentration on the
visual they could only have been worse.

The power of the Chaplin film comes from the expressiveness of
his pantomime. Mime is mute. To reveal the significant gestures and
facial flickers, Chaplin, as is his wont, uses the range of shots from full
to close. Only expository shots—the opening shots of the men trekking
North, the establishing shots of the dance hall, etc.—pull farther away
from the characters. Chaplin's unobtrusive editing consistently allows
the pantomime to play itself out without a cut—for example, the roll
dance.

The power of the Keaton film comes from the contrast between his
simple efforts and the immense problem surrounding him. Keaton, the
character, is as tight-lipped as he is expressionless. His character is essentially mute. His blank stare says everything that can be said about
the chaos he sees. To reveal the contrast of man and chaos, Keaton, as
is his wont, uses the range of shots between full and extreme long. His
camera works farther away from the characters than Chaplin's, consistently comparing them with their surroundings. His cutting is
slightly quicker than Chaplin's—to increase the pace and to reveal the
different perspectives of man and environment—but never so quick
or obtrusive as to make the stunts seem faked. With such control of
physical business, of thematic consistency, of appropriate structure,
of placement of the camera, and of functional editing, neither *The
Gold Rush* nor *The General* requires speech to speak.

The Circus (1928)
ALEXANDER BAKSHY

◆◆

Looking at our great and incomparable Charlie Chaplin I feel like
patting myself on the back. Did I not argue as long as fifteen years
ago that the ordinary "legitimate" actors should be barred from the

From "Charlie Chaplin" by Alexander Bakshy, Nation 126 (February 29, 1928): 247–48.

motion picture? It was of these actors that I said in 1913: "Are they aware that the cinematograph play is the most abstract form of the pantomime? Do they realize that if there is any stage on which the laws of movement should reign supreme, it is the cinematograph stage? If they did they would not have monopolized the cinematograph play, but would have left it to the dancers, clowns, and acrobats who do know something about the laws of movement." A few years later came Charlie, the perfect clown and acrobat, and by way of confirming my dictum at once leapt to such heights of artistic distinction that ever since there have been only two kinds of motion-picture actors: Charlie Chaplin and the rest. The classification is based not only on the singularity of Chaplin's genius, but equally so on the singularity of his methods as an actor. This fact, however, is often ignored. Chaplin's mannerisms, the peculiar traits of the screen character he has created, have been imitated and plagiarized times without number. On the other hand, his consistent pantomime acting (I cannot recall a single picture in which Chaplin moves his lips as if actually speaking), his emphasis on expressive movement (his gait, for instance), and his puppetlike, essentially nonrealistic treatment of his role—these are the characteristics of Chaplin's acting which have found but few imitators, and certainly none to show anything like Chaplin's appreciation of their meaning and importance.

In *The Circus*, his latest picture, Chaplin is again at his very best. His inexhaustible comic imagination has provided the picture with a more than ample supply of sidesplitting "stunts" of characteristic Chaplinesque quality, the most striking of these being the scenes at Noah's Ark and the lion's cage. The "big scene" of the picture, in which Charlie performs some amazing feats in tightrope walking (with the help of an attached wire), is funny too, but suffers somewhat from the attempt to join the wistful buffoonery of Charlie's little trick to the cruder and different fun of his helplessness in disengaging himself from the attacking monkeys. And through all these mirth-provoking scenes there flits the unforgettable image which has so endeared itself to the world—the image of a childishly simple and quixotically noble Pierrot who occasionally borrows the impishness of Harlequin.

In *The Circus* Chaplin's is a solo performance. The rest of the actors are not more than competent, and the direction of the picture as a whole lacks distinction. This last feature is disappointing. Chaplin showed his mettle as director in *A Woman of Paris*, and though there is no place for realism of this kind in his own grotesqueries, there is place in them for something which he is preeminently fitted to accomplish. His style of acting and all his dramatic upbringing proclaim Chaplin for what he actually is; a superb vaudeville comedian. We have motion pictures that are equivalent to comedy and drama.

But we still have no motion-picture vaudeville, i.e., entertainment shunning illusionist effects and making its appeal direct to the audience simply and solely as entertainment. I cannot help hoping that perhaps one day Chaplin will turn his mind to this richly promising field of experimental effort. There is waiting for him a full-size job worthy of his genius.

City Lights and Modern Times: Skirmishes with Romance, Pathos, and Social Significance
DONALD W. McCAFFREY

◆◆◆

The public's love for Chaplin manifested itself when he produced the silent film *City Lights* in 1931. By realizing a profit and achieving critical approval, the picture demonstrated that even though the industry had largely switched to sound (there were still some silent versions of talkies for remote provinces), the audience still relished the Little Tramp in pantomime. Chaplin accomplished a more spectacular feat when he produced *Modern Times* in 1936 with only a few concessions to the sound medium. By that time a battery of new comedians was creating talkies and the public enjoyed a gamut of comedy that ranged from the musical to the genteel to the folksy comedy-drama to the antisentimental concoctions of W. C. Fields and the Marx Brothers.

Two works clinging to the silent screen comedy tradition were released on the market by Chaplin in this age of chattering, verbal, gag-filled movies. The two films have some aspects in common, but also some differences that merit examination. Both present a bit of the romantic glow of the past by unfolding the genteel love affairs of the Little Tramp; they contain what critics are inclined to call Chaplin's blend of "pathos and comedy"; and they both attempt themes with sociopolitical significance. *City Lights* and *Modern Times*, therefore, provide a basis for comparison that cannot be found in any two of Chaplin's other films.

Although the romantic intrigues of the little fellow may be the portion of these pictures that will age and fade in value with time, they provide the basis for the total structure of the films. Neither film has a particularly effective story line, but the viewer today may excuse this weakness if he considers the virtues of the film—Chaplin's outstanding acting skills and his comic invention.

City Lights exhibits the most sentimental love affair—the little man's affection for a blind girl, a subject also employed by Harry Langdon in *The Strong Man* (1926). Although Chaplin's treatment of such a tear-jerking subject may offend some,[1] I believe the comedian directed and acted this portion of the film with restraint and good taste. The final moments of the film (often praised by critics), for example, show an effective underplaying of emotion. Simple dialogue and a poignant close-up show Chaplin avoiding the excesses of sentimental drama. Furthermore, an evaluator should allow the use of somewhat hoary material if it is handled well and if the total quality of the film overshadows its defects.

Although the romantic link of the Little Tramp with a poor orphaned girl in *Modern Times* may seem too Dickensesque for a twentieth-century drama and although the title seems to conflict with such an intrigue, the material may not have appeared so remote in 1936. The film was created at the height of the depression, when viewers needed only to look around them to see many poor little girls and many men who existed as homeless vagabonds without work or food.[2] This portion of the plot, like similar portion of *City Lights*, becomes important enough to congeal the total dramatic movement of the film. Also, we accept the relationship of the girl (played by Paulette Goddard) with the little fellow as valid because the acting of the two leading roles remains fresh and spontaneous when viewed today. This type of relationship in both films becomes an important counterpoint to the strong slapstick comedy. Working within the serious context of these affairs is a genteel form of comedy that was used by other comedians, but Chaplin's rivals seldom employed the sentimental so effectively to gain sympathy for their comic characters.

The serious aspects of *City Lights* and *Modern Times* lean heavily on the Little Tramp's relationships with the women (labeled simply

[1] See George Jean Nathan's article in this volume, pp. 79–81. This view might be considered a reaction merely to *City Lights*, but Nathan sets his guns on all of Chaplin's work up to that date.

[2] The reader should note Winston Churchill's interesting view of the tramp syndrome in the U.S. at that time. See his "Everybody's Language" in the second section of this volume.

"The Blind Girl" and "A Gamin"). Virginia Cherrill portrays the lovely, soulful girl next door—someone who would be superior to Charlie if she had her sight. The essence of the "pathos" in the film rests on this relationship. The girl has a vision of a rich, handsome man, instead of a little outcast. After recovering her sight at the end of the picture—the climactic scene—she touches the hand of the person she thinks is a strange little hobo and realizes the truth. It becomes one of the most tender moments on the screen. But it is also important to note that the little man's battle to survive on the fringe of society creates sympathy in another way. In the portrayal of the rich playboy (Harry Meyers) who loves Charlie when intoxicated but rejects him as an inferior being when sober, we see an excellent juxtaposition of the humorous and the serious. Some of the most effective comedy of the film develops when Charlie and the millionaire "do the town," and the rejection that takes place the next morning contains that blend of the humorous and serious that has made Chaplin so unique as a comedian.

The gamin heroine of the 1936 feature provides another blend of the serious and the comic. When Charlie suffers the pain of poverty, he has a companion in the girl. Partners against the establishment—the factory owners and those who control the hiring of employees—these two set up housekeeping in a little shack that is collapsing from faulty craftsmanship and decay. This brief scene illustrates the humor of attempted dignity even while the table, chairs, and walls of their home conspire against them by falling apart. Their childlike joy in a midnight seizure of a department store with all its luxuries provides light, gay comedy but also portrays the pathetic elements of their plight. Charlie has been given a night watchman's job, but ends up botching it and leaving the store a shambles because he gets drunk with the men who are trying to burglarize it. In fact, many portions of the two pictures develop such situations as this by blending the comic and the pathetic.

This analysis, it should be realized, is not a thorough evaluation of the comedy of the two pictures. Such scenes are obvious and have been discussed by others. *City Lights* has a brilliant comic boxing match; *Modern Times* portrays a burlesque of the assembly line that has never been equalled.[3] Both pictures abound in short comic routines and touches that provide the essence of Chaplin's humor—the type that he exhibited from his early days with Mack Sennett.

Finally, this examination of the comedian's two feature films leads to another comparison—one that may be found in the sociopolitical implications of the films. Some critics may see both works as satires,

[3] See pp. 152–56 of this volume for a scenario of this sequence.

but I believe the treatment focuses more clearly on human, individual values—a striving for human dignity in a cold world. A general, in some ways universal, statement develops. No clear-cut cry for social reform ever gets off the ground. Chaplin was not a satirist—he never had the sting of Ben Jonson or Molière—though he attempted satire in *Monsieur Verdoux* (1947). Critic Brooks Atkinson expresses the view that if Chaplin offered his film *Modern Times* "as social philosophy it is plain that he has hardly passed his entrance examinations, his comment is so trivial." [4] He continues by explaining that Chaplin's character always needed a hostile world to develop his comedy and that the actor-director had found one in the factory.

Although Chaplin never reached the sharp point of satire, he did use some ingredients of this form of humor. Police involvement in strike-breaking during the labor movement of the thirties had a grim undercurrent that made Chaplin's comic treatment of them sharper than his humor of the past. Reissuing *Modern Times* in the late sixties and early seventies has revealed that college students find a ready-made parallel to the treatment they are sometimes given by the law. *City Lights* offers no such parallel. The little man's up-and-down relationship with the drunk, then sober, millionaire remains a personal comment on human values without the social significance that *Modern Times* attempts, but never clearly achieves.

Both films have the vitality that make them living comedy classics. In an age of antisentimental humor, the tone of Buster Keaton's works is receiving increasing critical acclaim because he never allowed his little man to develop a full-fledged tear. But the sentimental qualities of Chaplin's comedy will never condemn his films. An extreme antisentimental age may find fault with parts of his films, but never with the total. His comedies present a full spectrum of humor. If one part will not suit a particular age's taste, another will. The older, more typical comedy of the formative age of the silent screen will always be appreciated in any future world. The flair of the master did not fade with the assault of sound. We can be grateful that he did defy the talkies with these works, for he gave us two examples of the best of the silent screen tradition.

[4] Brooks Atkinson, "Beloved Vagabond," *New York Times*, 16 February 1936, sec. 9, p. 1, cols. 1–3.

The Great Dictator (1940)
HERMAN G. WEINBERG

❖❖

The Great Dictator begins and ends on a note of terror. Starkly it opens on that fateful morning of November 11, 1918, somewhere on the Western front. The earth shakes with paroxysm, coughs, strangles, and vomits its gorge as the screaming shells plow into it, burst, and send the hot iron shrapnel flying in all directions from the roseate irises of foul black and red, like poisonous flowers laughing hysterically in their death agony, rising slowly in putrescent grandeur, infecting the sweet, cool morning air with its gangrenous vapor. (Elsewhere, the knife-glitter of the surgery ward, the torn flesh on the beds of pain, cotton soaked in ether, the clotted blood, twisted faces, and mingled stink of sweat, tetanus, and carbolic acid.) Behind the cold, gray opening of *The Great Dictator*, etched sketchily in charcoal blacks and whites of a gun here, a bursting shell there, and men scurrying like rats in a trench all around, is Latzko's *Men in War* and the hatred of war of the artist who begins here to make his plea for universal brotherhood.

When the camera swings swiftly by "Big Bertha," the obscene product of a diseased imagination, a little man, cog number "x" in the horrendous war machine now got out of control, stands ready to pull the lever-cord that will send a shell hurtling seventy miles to Paris on the Cathedral of Notre Dame. What an achievement! What a thing is man, indeed! But the little man by the big gun is Charlie Chaplin and so with an exquisite *pas de seul* he pulls the lever-cord and the shell spits out of the gun to land on a nearby outhouse, with a boom and a splintering crash, and a "pshaw!" with a dissappointed snap of the fingers from Chaplin. From this moment on Chaplin ridicules war. The spectator's horror has turned to bitter laughter. Chaplin struggles with a hand grenade that has fallen down his sleeve into the

From Saint Cinema: Selected Writings, 1929–1970, *by Herman G. Weinberg (New York: Drama Book Specialists, 1970), pp. 95–99. Reprinted by permission of Drama Book Specialists, New York.*

recesses of his uniform. "Take the pin out, count ten, and throw it!" he was warned. But with the pin out it is now sputtering somewhere in his clothing. Frantically he tears at his uniform as the precious seconds tick off, locates it, tosses it quickly away, and it explodes. With a sigh of relief, he faints. This is not war as the dictators teach it to their youth.

So Chaplin begins *The Great Dictator* by reviling war and showing his contempt for it as a thing of vast and horrible imbecility.

Wounded, he spends the next fifteen years in a hospital, emerging to find his fatherland held in thrall by a dictator heading a political party that has terrorized an entire nation into whimpering submission. He returns to his little barber shop, to take up life where he left it, but the street has now become a ghetto and the other Jews live in constant fear of the storm troopers. It seems that Jews have become the special butt of the new regime and his first encounter with storm troops who paint "Jew" over his shop windows leads to a fight and a realization that something terrible has happened while he has been away.

Then we see what it is that has happened. Before a great throng against banners with their ridiculous arbitrary insignia (Chaplin humorously substitutes the double-cross for the swastika), the great dictator himself. Again, Chaplin—the dictator, who had the misfortune to look like the little Jewish barber. (None of the reviewers of the film have commented on the beautiful logic of this resemblance in Chaplin's scenario; how it is borne out in real life that the world's most hated figure is indicted by the world's most loved figure.) Then follows a devastating parody of Hitler having a seizure, in other words, giving a speech. The psychopathic sobbings, breast beating, contemptuous exhortations for sacrifice which the fatherland demands, and all the assorted razzle-dazzle and pure, unadulterated sheep dip, have been scrambled by Chaplin into such a towering edifice of hilarious nonsense that at his conclusion, when the great dictator has shouted himself dry, Chaplin makes his final crushing comment on the whole paranoiac performance. The dictator gulps down a drink of water and then . . . but perhaps you had better see for yourself how deliciously Chaplin puts across one of the things he thinks is the matter with Hitler. ("My speech makes as much sense as his do [sic]," commented Chaplin recently.) Subsequently, there is another bit with the dictator again having shrieked himself hoarse, raising the glass of water spontaneously to his ear, but, suddenly realizing that what he regarded up to now as his *Sitzfleisch* was really only a hole in the ground, brings the glass down to his mouth. (But if you think Chaplin lets it go at that, you just don't know Chaplin, nor, for that matter, do you know the very funny story of the lunatic and the Queen of the

Netherlands that refugees brought over in recent weeks. If you know
the story, you'll know what I mean when you see this episode in the
film.)

"Originality and truth are to be found only in details," said Sten-
dhal. If I dwell on the details of Chaplin's great fresco, it is only because in them truth is revealed in all its splendid incandescence; in
these seemingly insignificant details are Chaplin's sharpest observations and, by far, his greatest originality. Such as, following upon an
autoerotic tête-à-tête with his minister of propaganda who envisions
for him a beautiful, blonde Aryan world ruled by a brunette dictator
whom this race of supermen and superwomen would worship as a
god, the great dictator leaps in ecstasy across the room and up a drapery, where he remains, for a moment poised and transfigured. In what
way is this merciless observation of Chaplin's different essentially
from the mystic of Berchtesgaden, perched in his armored aviary on
a high crag of the Bavarian Alps, there brooding on the *Goetter-
dammerung* he has unleashed on the world? ("I hear a beating of
wings!" said Herod. "I do not wish to hear it! It is an omen of death!"
Oscar Wilde would have understood Hitler, as Freud did. But the
beating of wings is the RAF and they understand him, too, as do now
even his former appeasers and as soon everyone will understand him.)

The dictator slides down the drapery, he is alone. He approaches
a terrestrial globe, lifts it—and flings it rapturously into the air. A
beatific smile plays upon his mouth. Against soft, shimmering music
out of Wagner by way of a good Aryan pogrom, the great dictator
does a bubble dance with the terrestrial globe. The *morbidezza* of this
scene, the profundity with which Chaplin, with shocking suddenness,
has realized the essence, not only of his own film, but of what is happening to the world today because of the aberration of one man, is
apocalyptic. It is not only the most intense lyrical moment that Chaplin has ever touched, but one has really to go back to Shakespeare and
Goethe to find passages that will equal it in its febrile glow.

The rest of the film's story, of how the little Jewish barber, after a
series of misadventures, comes to be mistaken for the "Furore" and is
called upon to speak before a massed throng come to "celebrate" the
fall of Austria, is too well known by now to need detailing here. The
critical boys and girls of the metropolitan press have had their field
day with this passionate summing up by Chaplin of how he feels
about the spectacle of humanity being kicked around. But Chaplin,
himself, has answered his critics better than I, or anyone, could do.
"May I not be excused in pleading for a better world? . . . It was a
very difficult thing to do. It would have been much easier to have the
barber and Hannah disappear over the horizon, off to the promised
land against the glowing sunset. But there is no promised land for the

oppressed people of the world. There is no place over the horizon to which they can go for sanctuary. They must stand and we must stand."

Listen to the closing words of Chaplin in *The Great Dictator*, that bitter four-minute speech in which he says, "I should like to help every one, if possible, Jew, Gentile, black man, white. We all want to help one another. Human beings are like that. We want to live by each other's happiness. . . . In the seventeenth chapter of St. Luke it is written: 'The Kingdom of God is within man'—not in one man nor a group of men, but in all men. You, the people, have the power to make this life free and beautiful, to make this life a wonderful adventure. . . ." Listen to these words and then contemplate the crowning irony of the National Legion of Decency's statement that they are not recommending *The Great Dictator* for children because: "Unrelated to plot or characterization, Chaplin utters a seemingly gratuitous and personal remark suggesting his disbelief in God. In view of the star's following, this utterance in its possible harmful effect on audiences is deplored." (Hannah, played by Paulette Goddard, asks the barber if he believes in God, and the barber thinks for a moment and begins, "Well . . ." but she interrupts him and goes on to tell him an incident apropos.)

I say here and now that every child in America should see *The Great Dictator*, that God is not the special concern (nor the private property) of the National Legion of Decency, that Chaplin's God is as good as theirs, that the godhead in man is a more real God than the detached Being that any individual or group of individuals can summon according to what axe he has to grind. Why did the Legion of Decency make no statement about the godlessness and bestiality of the Nazi film, *Feldzug in Polen,* which played for two months to packed and cheering houses in the German quarter of New York? What kind of "decency" is that?

In the Talmud it is written that there are things on earth which make even the angels in Heaven weep.

Monsieur Verdoux (1947)
ROGER MANVELL

◈◈

Monsieur Verdoux is the most bitterly satiric of Chaplin's films. Dean Swift in the bitterness of his view of human kind turned to the simplicity of the kingdom of the horses for a purge to sweeten his imagination. Swift took his satire to the very boundaries of ugliness: his art overbalanced into the pit of hatred. Chaplin in *Monsieur Verdoux* shows a keener edge to his satire than in any previous film. There is almost no pathos except in the revealing relationship between Verdoux and the lost girl whom he cannot bring himself to kill because she is at once too like himself and too unlike the human beings with whom he is at war. It is this satire, this comedy of murders as Chaplin calls it, which makes the action of the film as symbolic of Chaplin's state of mind as *Gulliver's Travels* was of Swift's. If you take the action of the film as its face value it is merely puzzling, a perverse story which seems to suggest that murder is funny, provided the women destroyed are eccentric types. The film has been unpopular with reviewers (I will not say with critics), and it has undoubtedly confused the public who know Chaplin only as a rather old-fashioned and sentimental funny man who used, if they are old enough, to make them laugh in their youth by the dexterity of his clowning. Why, they say, does he now ask us to laugh at murder? Why, they ask, does he come out of character, as it were, and pose awkward questions *at* the audience (in the closing speech of *The Great Dictator*) or make what appear to be deeply felt remarks about the world before his execution at the end of *Monsieur Verdoux*? This is wrong, they assume, in a comedian.

The answer to these questions is not so much that Chaplin himself

From The Film and the Public *by Roger Manvell (London: Penguin Books Ltd., 1955), pp. 166–70. Reprinted by permission of the publisher.*

has changed, as that the desperateness of these times has fortified him
to make his art an outspoken challenge to the aggressiveness of humanity. It is no longer a secret that Chaplin himself, British-born, became an isolated figure in America, unpopular as a person and per-
secuted within certain limits. His refusal to participate in any war
work accentuated the opposition to him. It is the old story; the artist
is acknowledged but his point of view disliked. Provided he will just
entertain, well and good, but his social criticism is unwelcome and
invites such reprisals and ostracism as can conveniently be brought to
bear. He has now left the States forever.

Monsieur Verdoux reflects all this. Verdoux is at war with society.
He is an ordinary man, simple in his tastes, married to a crippled wife
to whom he is devoted and living in an idealized little country cot-
tage. His mysterious "business" in the city does not rouse his wife's
curiosity: he is a most respectable citizen, reproving his son for cruelty
in some trifling offence. This is his true life, the life open to him only
so long as his security as a bank clerk remained. But the misfortunes
of our ill-organized and acquisitive society rob him of that security,
throw him permanently out of work, and force him to live on the
black market of his wits. He "marries" a series of women all of whom
are distasteful to him, and who pass their time living parasitic lives of
the kind which brought him face to face with his own insecurity as a
wage-earner. He murders them in turn and takes the spoils, returning
always to support his little family in the country.

In his criminal conduct he is always disciplined, meticulous, and
practical. He is at war, as much a craftsman as a general, killing with
as little compunction and taking the resulting booty to support life as
he thinks it should be ordered. Here the satire of the central theme is
lightened into comedy, and the gay tricks of Chaplin's clowning, always more perfect in the rhythm of their timing than anything of the
kind yet known upon the screen, take over. But not for long. The
incinerator smokes at the bottom of the garden, or the moon shines
while Chaplin stands poised with delicate hands outstretched to kill,
his pantomime on the verge of becoming a macabre ballet.

Verdoux is therefore the natural man dehumanized by the un-
natural cruelties which are slowly strangling the civilized world. He
bears the comic exaggeration of the satiric form, like Swift's characters
or those of Molière. Two women soften his hard attitude to the world
—his wife and the lost girl played by Marilyn Nash. Although the
girl is destitute she retains an unquestioning belief in the goodness
of human nature. Chaplin shows that Verdoux cannot resist the appeal of such a faith when she so openly expects him to share it. It is
notable that while Verdoux is still in doubt whether he will use the
girl as a human test for the strength of his poisoned wine, there is only

conversation and the tension of action in silence; when the appeal to his kindliness has succeeded and the threat to her is removed, then music is introduced. The harmony of nature is restored, the balance of humanity achieved.

Chaplin could have redeemed Verdoux from this point had he so wished, and had the Hays Code allowed him to do so. But Chaplin did not choose to redeem him. By a fortuitous blow Verdoux loses his family in some outburst of social violence which Chaplin does not trouble to explain but which is due to the economic and political crises of the thirties. He is left to shift for himself, alone and more deeply embittered than ever. When he meets the lost girl once more he finds she is the kept woman of a rich manufacturer of munitions. Beauty and faith have been sold to the destroyer. Verdoux is aged and poverty-stricken: he sees no reason for prolonging life or humanity. Her faith, however, is not yet destroyed. "Life is beyond reason," she tells him, "that's why we must go on." But Verdoux allows himself to be arrested.

The last section brings to a head the philosophy of the film. No stress is laid on the process of the trial except Verdoux's last remark after his death sentence: "I shall see you all very soon." Society is merely destroying him just in advance of destroying itself. In his prison cell he is interviewed by the press; now that he is notorious space in the newspapers is at his disposal. He tells the reporter that "crime does not pay in a small way," that robbery and murder are the natural expression of "these criminal times." "That's business," he says. War is the outcome of it all. "One murder makes a villain, millions a hero."

To the priest who comes to escort him to the place of execution he declares, "I am at peace with God, my conflict is with man." When the priest prays that God have mercy on his soul, he replies lightly, "Why not; after all it belongs to him." He hesitates over a glass of rum and decides to have it, as he has never tasted rum before. There is something superb about this moment before death, elemental like the loosening of Lear's button. It unites the soul with the body for the last time. Then with the curious ritual which attends all scenes of death, he goes out, a small man with sloping, aged shoulders walking into the prison courtyard to heavy music. This time there is no long road to the horizon, no pretty girl for companion, no pathetic fatalism. It is a stark march to death.

In most criticism of *Monsieur Verdoux* this essential philosophy of the film has been overlooked or avoided. Reviewers have said the film is unequal, that it is not very funny, that its comedy is spoilt by the intrusion of Chaplin's personal point of view, or that it is a film of many brilliant and inimitable moments, mostly moments of superb pantomime with such skilful players as Martha Raye. The general impression is that what respect has been accorded to *Monsieur Verdoux* is a respect born of the traditional praise of Chaplin the comedian. No film which attempts so much double meaning could probably escape some faults; the comic pantomime at times seems pushed to the point of irrelevance, like the overbalanced byplay of a Lenten holiday. There are episodes such as the long action of Verdoux's avoidance of one wife who turns up at the reception held before his marriage to another, where the delicate touch of Clair would have been more appropriate. That almost all the aphorisms are kept for the end of the film is appropriate to the scene in the death cell, but robs the last sequences of some emotion; Verdoux becomes one with his creator. But these are small faults compared with the courageous achievement of the work as a whole, which is the most serious of all Chaplin's films. It points ahead to an even more important film should Chaplin care to develop and perfect his messianic style in another profoundly felt social satire.

The Lineage of *Limelight*

WALTER KERR

◆◆

One of the marks of homage we pay to a major artist is that we follow his best, his middling, and his poorest appearances with equal curiosity, if not with equal satisfaction. We do not make the production of a masterpiece the condition of our attendance upon his newest work; it is enough that he is working. Thus, for me—now that *Limelight* is here—it is ample satisfaction simply to *see* Chaplin again. Though the film runs a good two-and-a-half hours, I would have no great difficulty in sticking out another two-and-a-half without flinching. If I bring an excess of affection and respect with me, the affection and respect have been earned a thousand times; if the new film tends to draw on these things in order to sustain it, I am happy enough to

From Theatre Arts *36 (November 1952): 73–75. Reprinted by permission of Walter Kerr.*

hand them over. Chaplin *can* do wrong; but he cannot be uninteresting.

And *Limelight* contains a good many things which carry their own weight. The climactic vaudeville sketch in which Chaplin is assisted by Buster Keaton is very funny. Chaplin has a delightful passage-at-arms with a hobgoblin landlady. Again and again the actor rescues a scene headed for bathos with a tart flash of honesty. And, perhaps most of all, he has made the interior excitement of suceeding in the theater seem real and moving: when a ballerina takes her first trial spin across a deserted stage some mysterious insight asserts itself and you know why you love this absurd profession.

But the fascination which these fragments hold for someone who is long since committed to Chaplin is quite different from the cool objectivity which must be pursued by the practicing critic. And—though no reviews have appeared at this writing—it is fairly clear that *Limelight* is in for trouble.

At first sight the difficulties which may be in store for Chaplin would seem to stem from his decision to produce an essentially serious, predominantly pathetic film in which there are—quite intentionally —only isolated bits of comedy. The old dream of Hamlet has come home to roost, we are tempted to think; the great clown has betrayed himself into an overambitious exercise in self-pity. And there are certainly moments in *Limelight* which smack so strongly of the confessional as to give support to this view.

I don't believe, though, that the problem of *Limelight* can be resolved so simply, or that the film can be distinguished from the main body of Chaplin's work in terms of its seriousness, its "artiness," or its sentimentality. The sentimentality has always been there, though in the past it was usually balanced by a last-minute, face-saving comic shock; the comparative artiness of some of the photography is preferable to the harsh, flat, and old-fashioned grays which marked his last few films; and there is nothing here to say conclusively that Chaplin is incapable of a first-rate serious performance.

In spite of a certain uncomfortable coziness between Chaplin and Chaplin which runs through the film, there are many well-acted moments: the candid shame with which he accepts a loan from an old friend; the sharp tongue which he cannot still when he is offered a job he needs; the half-happy, half-stunned bewilderment of his discovery that his protegé is a better dancer than he had quite anticipated; the mocking, incredulous shrug with which he accepts an ironic dismissal from a ballet company. He has, in addition, directed the other actors well: Claire Bloom, Nigel Bruce, and son Sidney Chaplin give firm, confident, plausible performances.

What sets *Limelight* completely apart from the Chaplin tradition, and what damages it most seriously, is not its pretentious flirtation with weight, but its hopeless capitulation to words. The man who originally fought the coming of sound, who dared to produce at least two silent films long after sound had triumphed, and who, even when be began to speak, still struggled to keep the mobile image dominant over the sound track, has changed his mind. He has not only gone over to what he once considered the enemy; he has gone over with love.

From the first reel of *Limelight* it is perfectly clear that Chaplin now wants to talk, that he *loves* to talk, that in this film he intends to do little *but* talk. Where a development in the story line might easily be conveyed by a small visual effect, he prefers to make a speech about it. Where the 1917 music-hall background obviously opens the door to extensive onstage pantomime, he prefers to stand still and sing a song. This is not a compromise between the old and the new, an adjustment to inevitable and necessary change; it is a disturbing rejection of the nature of the medium itself.

Limelight has to do with a fading old vaudevillian who prevents a young dancer's suicide, who nurses the hysterically paralytic girl back to health in his own room, and who finally gives her the self-confidence she needs to work again. In an earlier Chaplin film we might have been sure of at least two scenes: one in which the unskillful and embarrassed Samaritan attempts to set up the sort of light housekeeping which will take care of the girl's needs, at first making a glorious mess of it and then suddenly and ingeniously making it all come out right (*The Kid, Modern Times*); and another in which he attempts to cheer her up with an inspirational little homily, *acted out* (David and Goliath in *The Pilgrim,* the effort to entertain the girls in *The Gold Rush*). Sound does not preclude the possibility of dramatizing these situations; it simply adds a dimension to be used or dismissed at will. In *Limelight* it is the dramatization which has been dismissed. Mr. Chaplin simply lectures the girl, out loud and at great length. The content is entirely verbal.

Nor need the fact that this is no longer the little tramp necessarily inhibit the use of pantomime. Mr. Chaplin is playing a seedy and impoverished former music-hall entertainer with a reputation for clowning; the realistic preparation is all there. Nor, finally, would the inevitably comic quality of such improvization in any way undercut the pathos which Mr. Chaplin is after; the pathos would be intensified at every turn (*City Lights*).

Take another, less extensive example. Chaplin tells the girl he is about to have an interview with a man who may employ him. He does not know what attitude to take: the condescending manner of a man who is regularly employed, or the supplicating manner of one who hasn't eaten in weeks. It is inconceivable that Chaplin should have been able to resist the impulse to act out both attitudes for the girl; but he has resisted it. There is, to be sure, some faint facial play as he talks out the problem, some hint of mimicry. But we are denied anything more graphic than this. The burden of the scene must rest on the dialogue, and the impulse to illustration is forever chilled.

From being that genius who brought the form of the motion picture to its purest realization, Mr. Chaplin has moved to the logical opposite: he is no longer a man interested in making a *motion* picture at all. An inspired visual scenarist has become an indifferent playwright. There is nothing in *Limelight* which might not have been written for the stage, though it might bettter have been written in the heyday of the late Austin Strong.

Since Chaplin was, from the outset, painfully aware of the pitfalls of sound, how is it that he has now fallen so wholeheartedly into its deepest trap, its final excess? I think the answer lies in Chaplin's image of himself as philosopher.

It has always been known that the great Charlie fancied his talents as a speculative thinker. Nearly every study of Chaplin—from Sam Goldwyn's cursory *The Real Chaplin* of 1923 to Theodore Huff's extended *Charlie Chaplin* of last year—remarks on his enthusiasm for "intellectual" conversation, his passionate pursuit of minds reputed to be superior in one way or another, his anxiety to meet them on their own level and, what is more, on their own subjects. Most such studies also manage to imply, in however roundabout terms, that the artist's enthusiasm tends to exceed his equipment.

Chaplin was perfectly able to resist the inroads of sound on his work as a comedian. (He didn't make an actual talking film until twelve or thirteen years after the sound revolution, and he was much praised for the manner in which he originally subordinated sound track to image.) What he apparently can no longer resist is the opportunity presented by sound to display the other, and hitherto hidden, side to his personality—his desire to be known as a thinker. He was undoubtedly encouraged in this by the vocabulary which his most ardent admirers had long used to describe his best work, a vocabulary which held the little tramp "profound," the tramp's adventures "shot through with significance," and the tramp's creator a "multiple genius."

But the difference between a visual profundity and a verbal one is very great. One is achieved intuitively, by implying layers of *unspoken* meaning behind a simple picture. The other speaks out its meaning in a series of logical equations which require no picture at all. (Thus, what Chaplin does *not* say at the end of *City Lights* is dazzling with meaning; all that he does say throughout the first half of *Limelight* is literal, explicit, and without esthetic life.)

The intuitive and the rational methods of getting at truth are anti-
thetical methods which tend to fight one another. Rarely—very rarely
—do we find the two highly developed, side by side, in a single personality. For Chaplin the switch-over was bound to be dangerous; in a
predominantly pictorial medium it was almost sure to be disastrous.

The split between the artist and the thinker began with the closing
moments of *The Great Dictator*. Throughout the first three quarters
of that film the content—whether purposefully satirical or merely
antic—is conveyed in mobile, lifelike images. The dictator does not
make a speech to say that he covets the world: he dances with the
globe in his hands. No one announces that the great new world order
is somehow defective: a train persistently stops at the wrong place.
Meanwhile an anonymous little barber shaves his customer to the
rhythms of a Hungarian dance.

As the film progresses, the illiterate little barber is mistaken for the
paranoid leader. At its climax, after a few preliminary comic misadventures, he is called upon to address the assembled nation. He hesitates. Then, looking directly into the camera, the figure before us
launches into a long, literate harangue on the merits of political democracy. The figure is no longer anyone we recognize. It is patently
not that of the barber we have fondly followed all evening; no pretense is made that the barber might be capable of such a speech. No
explanation is offered because none is possible. We have simply and
suddenly been introduced to the other Chaplin—Chaplin the thinker
—in the intimacy of his living room. As though this first shock were
not enough, another is in store for us: the speech is dreadful. It is a
hoary collection of disorganized platitudes, belligerently delivered.
Not only the barber has disappeared. Chaplin the artist has disappeared. The film has disappeared.

The Great Dictator need not have ended in this way, not even to
make its point. The old Charlie would at least have given us an
enemy plane dumping a bundle of propaganda leaflets onto Charlie's
head; Charlie's girl friend Hannah laboriously spelling out words and
phrases for him; and a final speech—halting, helpless, heartfelt—in
which the little barber does his desperate best to reconstruct this beautiful dream, filling out in gesture which he cannot force into words.
A speech in character might have been comic in its confusion and in-
finitely more touching in its earnest simplicity.

Chaplin's subsequent work stems directly from the last five minutes,
and the worst five minutes, of *The Great Dictator*. The actor announced that *Monsieur Verdoux* was to have moral value: "Von
Clausewitz said that war is the logical extension of diplomacy; M. Verdoux feels that murder is the logical extension of business." Given the
intellectual posturing of this premise, it was no surprise to find the

film degenerating into a thesis-piece whose point was "stated verbally by Chaplin in the bluntest possible terms and with a bitterness of intonation carrying with it, astonishingly enough, a grain or two of smugness" (Parker Tyler in *The Kenyon Review*).

Limelight has not the thesis structure of *Verdoux*, but it is ripe with random observations on Freud, life, love, nature, and fame. The language is—especially during the long first half—uncomfortably cosmic; the camera is steadily focused on Chaplin's mind. And there is finally a line of dialogue which summarizes the actor's whole latter-day development.

At one point the adoring dancer turns to the philosophical clown and says:

"To hear you talk no one would ever think you were a comedian."

Now this isn't just one of those unlucky lines that offers the reviewers an opening for sarcasm. It is much more than that, because Chaplin is ahead of the reviewers. He knows that the line is a dangerous one. He anticipates its dangers by reacting to it with mock dismay, with irony. Yet he will not part with it. He secretly hopes that, once he has made light of the whole business, the audience will still be impressed with the things a comedian can say when he puts his mind to it. He wants a disclaimer of intellectuality and an insistence upon intellectuality at one and the same moment. He is conscious of his present course, self-conscious about his present course, and determined upon his present course.

There are wheels within wheels here, but it might have been better had they never been set turning. A profound clown—the greatest, most beloved we have—is seeking a second reputation as a sage. It is not likely to equal his first.

Scenario Extracts

In recent times scholars of the motion-picture classics have made detailed examinations of the incidents that take place in film drama. Shot-by-shot scenarios are sometimes prepared for a more accurate study of the works.

Here are three excerpts, prepared by the editor, from comedies that show some of the facets of Chaplin's humor. An elaborate comedy routine created from simple, burlesque material is evident in the 1918 *Shoulder Arms*. Unique in its treatment of Chaplin's physical features, it shows the development of humor derived from the little man's splay feet.

A more genteel, human, comic tone is evident in the breakfast scene from *The Kid* (1921). In his feature films the comedian developed such touches as these—touches that revealed his skill in handling various types of humor.

Chaplin brought a full-blown silent-screen tradition into the sound era with an elaborate assembly-line sequence in *Modern Times*. One of the most effective (if not the best) sequences, it shows the wide range of comic invention that he could bring to one situation. Such innovation obviously has elevated him to such a height among comedians that he may be called the king of comedy.

OPENING SCENE FROM *Shoulder Arms*[1]

Title 1: The Awkward Squad.

1. LS CAMERA PANS FROM RIGHT TO LEFT ON SQUAD.
   A view of a line-up of soldiers who are facing front. In the left part of the frame Charlie stands in the line-up with his feet spread, a blank look on his face. The drill sergeant, far right, gives a manual of arms order:

   1. Charlie lowers the rifle to the wrong side (his left) hitting the toe of the soldier next to him. The soldier jumps up and

[1] A three-reel film released by First National in October 1918.

149

down, holding his foot. Charlie shifts his rifle to his right after being corrected by the sergeant.

2. Right arms ordered and the little fellow gets the weapon on his shoulder upside down. He is corrected again but gets the rifle on his *left* shoulder. Admonished once more, he finally gets the right position.

3. Order given to about face. All men execute the move correctly except Charlie—he merely walks (in small steps) to achieve the position. The sergeant has him step forward for instructions after another about face is executed with the same results. Charlie tries the action two times; the drill master then shows him how to point his toe behind him to carry out the action. The little fellow points his toe, throws out one arm and smiles broadly as if he were striking a pose before an admiring audience. Then he tries to turn but gets his legs twisted together and can't make the turn. Twisting more violently with each try, he almost falls down. He gives up, shrugging his shoulders in a childlike manner. The leader illustrates the move. Charlie puts his pointed toe in front instead of behind him. Finally, he gets it right after one more correction by his instructor. He marches back into ranks (with back to camera) and almost falls over as order is given to about face.

4. Order given to mark time. Charlie does it more vehemently than the others with his toes pointed out in his characteristic manner. The sergeant barks at him:

Title 2: "Put those feet in."

2. LS He looks down at his feet and turns them in so that he is marking time pigeon-toed. Evidently giving an order to mark right, the sergeant moves off right with the squad following him. Charlie, on the left counting time and looking at his feet as they assume their natural (distorted) position, tries to point them in. Suddenly realizing he has been left behind, he dashes off right.

3. LS Coming hurriedly into line from left frame background, he finds the squad standing still, now marking time. His hat falls off as he gets into line. As he picks it up, the group is ordered to go left, reversing their previous direction. The leader comes up to front of the line as the squad moves off left.

4. LS TRAVEL SHOT IN FRONT OF SOLDIERS AS THEY MARCH. A MODERATELY HIGH ANGLE SHOT.

As the group marches forward (toward camera), the sergeant tells Charlie to walk with his toes in. He marches pigeoned-toed for a short time, but his feet go back to the "natural" position. The leader points to his feet. Once more he pulls them in with the same results. The sergeant points (for the third time) to his feet, and poor Charlie goes into his awkward march—in position only briefly as he switches back to the typical spread. Orders given to halt.

5. LS Moving in from the right, the squad stops. Ordered to fall out, Charlie does a leaping little dance to his tent which is seen in the background—obviously happy the ordeal is over.

PANCAKE SCENE FROM *The Kid* [2]

195. LS Charlie is revealed sitting up in bed left, smoking a cigarette and reading. Kid at stove right is cooking. He stands on a small stool, stirring with a spoon.

196. CMS At the stove Kid pours batter into frying pan for pancakes. A big stack of cakes on the edge of stove in foreground. Kid taps spatula on stove, then breaks off a piece of pancake from the stack and nibbles.

197. MS Charlie still in bed reading paper, with a light air of dignity.

198. CMS Kid picks up stack of pancakes and moves left.

199. LMS He sets the cakes on the corner of the table and (with back to camera) calls to Charlie, who is in bed in background. With knife and fork in hand, Kid motions for him to come. He puts utensils down, puts hands on hips, and moves to background to get Charlie up from bed.

200. LS Going up to the bed, Kid yanks paper from Charlie and gets chair by bed. Charlie rubs hands together, yawns, stretches, and lifts foot up—it comes through a hole in the blanket. He sees foot and pulls it back under the cover.

201. LLS Charlie moves forward under blanket, which is now over his head. Suddenly, his head pops through the hole and he has an improvised robe. He works to the edge of the bed, stands up with dignity, and steps forward.

202. CU A view of Charlie's feet as he slides into his untied shoes with loose strings. Moves forward in the familiar duck waddle.

[2] Chaplin's first feature (six reels), released by First National in February 1921.

203. LS   Charlie moves right to stove, rubs hands together, and
            grabs chair near the stove.

204. MS   He moves it to table and sits down right. Kid on left
            pinches Charlie's cheek playfully and receives from his
            guardian a gentle gesture (finger to lip) to restrain himself.
            Charlie divides pancakes, counting them as if they were a
            deck of cards. He takes one from his own pile and cuts it
            in half, giving one part to Kid. Eager to dig in, the little
            boy is stopped by Charlie in order to give the blessing. He
            looks up slightly with eyes open and prays. Finished with
            the ritual, Kid starts eating. Charlie lifts a bite to his
            mouth; he stops, puts a huge piece of butter on the pan-
            cake, and folds it around the butter. He stops the boy from
            eating and tells him how to use his knife. Charlie puts
            syrup on his cakes and starts to eat.
            FADE TO BLACK—FADE IN.

205. CU   Plates are now empty. Kid beats with fork and knife on
            his plate.

206. MS   Charlie belches and hits his chest with fist—obviously un-
            comfortable after the meal. Kid goes off frame left and
            returns bringing a toy dog, kisses it, and pushes it to
            Charlie's cheek. Charlie kisses the toy half-heartedly. Kid
            then runs off left. Charlie scratches his right arm and
            belches.
            FADE TO BLACK

CHARLIE GOES MAD ON THE ASSEMBLY LINE:
A SEQUENCE FROM *Modern Times*[3]

Title 5: As time marches on into the late afternoon.

70. LS   At central control in the factory a young, muscular man
            without his shirt listens to the boss who orders, "More
            speed!" (voiced sound) on the closed-circuit television
            screen. The man turns a wheel and increases power, indi-
            cated by sound track.

71. MLS   Charlie, a big, heavy-set man with a mustache, and another
            man are working on the assembly-line belt. They work on
            a series of plates that have two bolts on them. Charlie uses
            two wrenches to tighten the bolts. Foreman comes in from
            left and urges him to work harder. Charlie sneezes and

[3] A feature released by United Artists in February 1936.

gets behind, missing a plate. Running after it, he makes a dive in its direction as the belt runs toward a chute. The big fellow grabs him by the heels to keep him from being fed into the chute. He calls:

Title 6: "He's crazy!!!"

72. CMS Charlie on the belt being pulled left. Desperately he tries to bolt the nuts on the plate down.

73. LMS The big guy holding onto his foot calls for help and lets go. Charlie goes down the belt and into the chute.

74. LLS He is then revealed going through an elaborate system of wheels and cogs from left to right. After moving up and over cogs and rollers, he ends up on the largest wheel, right.

75. LS A closer shot showing him on the huge cog as he tightens the bolts two by two on the wheel he is stretched on.

76. MLS A man turns a control wheel.

77. LLS We see Charlie going in reverse direction (right to left) of shot 74

78. LS We see him coming back from the chute still in the process of bolting down the nuts.

79. MS An amazed look on the big fellow's face as he looks down. (Charlie is off frame on the belt.)

80. LS Charlie gets up and swings wrenches around. He attempts to tighten up the breasts of the big guy—then heads for his nose. He goes down the line "bolting" two men who come up to him. He gives each of their noses a twist—first with right hand—then with left. Starts a light, gay, little dance as he comes back and tweaks the big fellow's nose once more. Then does his ballet step down the line when the boss's secretary comes in from left front. He stops and eyes her.

81. LS Charlie holds the wrenches down next to his ears and moves them up, more like horns. He wags them up and down with an ludicrous smile on his face.

82. LS He stares at her as she goes past him. She starts running, and he follows.
CAMERA TRAVELS WITH THEM.

83. LS Secretary running from back right along the time clock in the hallway. Charlie after her as they go off front and left.

84. **LS**   Coming from the shop onto the street, the secretary gets behind a water hydrant. Charlie obviously has been attracted by the large buttons on the back of her dress. Distracted by the huge bolts on the fire hydrant, he dives for them, and the secretary escapes into the shop again (to right and back).
CAMERA TRAVELS WITH WOMAN AS SHE COMES FORWARD.

85. **MS**   A matronly woman with huge breasts coming down the street. She has a series of large buttons on her dress—two on the tip of her breasts.

86. **LS**   She comes up to Charlie who is still at the hydrant. He sees her; she stops and is startled by the expression of glee on his face. She runs away (back left) with Charlie after her.
CAMERA TRAVELS WITH WOMAN RUNNING AWAY—SHE COMES TOWARD CAMERA.

87. **LS**   As woman runs, her large breasts bobbing, Charlie weaves back and forth behind her with his wrenches in hand.
PAN WITH WOMAN.

88. **LS**   She rounds a corner going left, and he comes after her. She runs up to a policeman and points at the little man.

89. **MLS**   Desperately she explains her plight to the officer and points forward.
PAN WITH CHARLIE AND POLICEMAN.

90. **LS**   The policeman runs after the little fellow as he dashes away and around the corner.

91. **LS**   Coming into frame up left and coming forward, he executes the famous skid on one foot as he goes into shop on right.

92. **LS**   Up near the time clock, Charlie stops, punches in, then throws card away as he runs to back of hall and left— skidding on one foot as he rounds another corner.

93. **LLS**   Into central control from off right (and front) he slides to the side of the shirtless young man. He watches him throw a couple of switches on left. Charlie goes with him and throws a few also (as if it were a game) and the young man, hard at work, pushes him back and tries to correct the damage Charlie has done. The little fellow moves to the switches, levers, and wheels, right.

94. **LS**   Charlie at the switches. He throws about six of them and presses his hands in front of himself in a childlike gesture

of pleasure. Moving to a big lever, he leans on it with gusto
—one leg flying behind him as he pushes the lever all the
way to the right.

95. LLS   Man on left and Charlie on right—both throwing switches.
In the background explosions come from the dynamos.

96. MS   Young man pointing at him, telling him not to throw any
more switches.

97. LLS   Young man runs to back and right to throw the switches
where they should be.

98. MLS   Charlie now has an oil-can with long spout. He squirts
the young man as he is in the process of correcting the
damage. Charlie dances gaily off front and left.

99. LMS   Boss in his office, pushing switches. Television screen in
background flashing with sputter of defective sound—
circuits blowing.

100. LS   Charlie enters from right. Dancing wildly, he comes back
to his assembly line.

PAN LEFT WITH HIM.

He squirts one of the men using a hammer on the plates.
Then he goes to the big fellow (screen left). He dances
forward and left.

101. LLS The assembly line now is shut down so the men can chase
him. He jumps over center of belt, comes back to a lever
(left), and throws it on. Men are forced to go back to work
—they are slaves of the moving belt. Charlie dances back
and right as they work. Belt now is shut off again, but
Charlie runs to lever and turns machine on. Once more the
men are forced to work. He runs off right and front.

102. LLS Dancing down another assembly line, Charlie squirts a
row of men; then he climbs a ladder in upper right background.

103. MLS At top of ladder he encounters a man and gives him a
shot of oil in the face as he grabs a huge chain and swings
down and off.

104. LLS He swings over heads of men and off up right.

105. LLS Men gather on floor of shop, looking up. Boss at right.
Big man from his assembly line unit with other men left.

106. LMS Charlie hangs onto a huge hook and chain dangling from
a crane. He points his oil-can down—a mad gaiety on his
face.

107. **LLS** Boss motions down with his arm. Hook and chain lowered. Charlie squirts oil in faces of boss and the big fellow.

108. **LS** Ambulance in from right. It stops in front of a shop entrance.

109. **LS** Big fellow and cop hustle Charlie out door of shop, holding him from the ground—forward and right.

110. **LS** They come to the ambulance, Charlie supported between them. He is walking in the air. They put him down before ambulance attendant, left.

111. **LMS** Attendant (left) gets a squirt of oil in the face from Charlie. Policeman takes oil-can from him, but Charlie gets a tiny oil-can from his pocket and squirts cop in the eyes.

PAN WITH ACTION—LEFT.

They hustle him into ambulance. It drives off center and back.

FADE TO BLACK.

Filmography

The following list of films does not attempt to present all available data on Chaplin's work. Thorough examinations of his movies can be found in *The Films of Charlie Chaplin*, by Gerald D. McDonald, et al. (New York: Citadel, 1965) or in *Charlie Chaplin,* pp. 313–31, by Theodore Huff (New York: Henry Schuman, 1951). The acting credits in this index have been condensed to include only those players who are most important in the history of the film or who relate most directly to the plot.

KEYSTONE FILM COMPANY—1914

(All films were produced under the supervision of Mack Sennett and most were photographed by Frank Williams.)

February

1. *Making a Living* (1 reel)
   Directed by Henry Lehrman.
2. *Kid Auto Races at Venice* (split-reel)
   Directed by Henry Lehrman.
3. *Mabel's Strange Predicament* (1 reel)
   Directed by Henry Lehrman and Mack Sennett.
   With Mabel Normand.
4. *Between Showers* (1 reel)
   Directed by Henry Lehrman.
   With Ford Sterling.

March

5. *A Film Johnnie* (1 reel)
   With Virginia Kirtley and Fatty Arbuckle.
6. *Tango Tangles* (1 reel)
   With Ford Sterling and Fatty Arbuckle.
7. *His Favorite Pastime* (1 reel)
   Directed by George Nichols.
   With Fatty Arbuckle.

8. *Cruel Cruel Love* (1 reel)

April

9. *The Star Boarder* (1 reel)
   With Edgar Kennedy and Alice Davenport.
10. *Mabel at the Wheel* (2 reels)
    Directed by Mack Sennett and Mabel Normand.
    With Mabel Normand and Chester Conklin.
11. *Twenty Minutes of Love* (1 reel)
    With Edgar Kennedy and Chester Conklin.
12. *Caught in a Cabaret* (2 reels)

May

13. *Caught in the Rain* (1 reel)
    Written and directed by Charles Chaplin.
    With Alice Davenport and Mack Swain.
14. *A Busy Day* (split-reel)
    Written and directed by Charles Chaplin.
    With Mack Swain.

June

15. *The Fatal Mallet* (1 reel)
    With Mabel Normand.
16. *Her Friend the Bandit* (1 reel)
    Directed by Charles Chaplin and Mabel Normand.
    With Mabel Normand and Charles Murray.
17. *The Knockout* (2 reels)
    With Fatty Arbuckle and Edgar Kennedy.
18. *Mabel's Busy Day* (1 reel)
    Directed by Mabel Normand and Charles Chaplin.
    With Mabel Normand.
19. *Mabel's Married Life* (1 reel)
    Directed by Charles Chaplin and Mabel Normand.
    With Mabel Normand.

July

20. *Laughing Gas* (1 reel)
    Written and directed by Charles Chaplin.

August

21. *The Property Man* (1 reel)
    Written and directed by Charles Chaplin.

22. *The Face on the Barroom Floor* (1 reel)
Directed by Charles Chaplin.

23. *Recreation* (split-reel)
Written and directed by Charles Chaplin.

24. *The Masquerader* (1 reel)
Written and directed by Charles Chaplin.
With Fatty Arbuckle and Charles Murray.

25. *His New Profession* (1 reel)
Written and directed by Charles Chaplin.
With Charley Chase.

September

26. *The Rounders* (1 reel)
Written and directed by Charles Chaplin.
With Fatty Arbuckle and Minta Durfee.

27. *The New Janitor* (1 reel)
Written and directed by Charles Chaplin.
With Al St. John.

October

28. *Those Love Pangs* (1 reel)
Written and directed by Charles Chaplin.
With Chester Conklin.

29. *Dough and Dynamite* (2 reels)
Written and directed by Charles Chaplin.
With Chester Conklin.

30. *Gentlemen of Nerve* (1 reel)
Written and directed by Charles Chaplin.
With Mabel Normand and Chester Conklin.

November

31. *His Musical Career* (1 reel)
Written and directed by Charles Chaplin.
With Mack Swain.

32. *His Trysting Place* (2 reels)
Written and directed by Charles Chaplin.
With Mabel Normand and Mack Swain.

33. *Tillie's Punctured Romance* (6 reels)
Directed by Mack Sennett.
Scenario by Hampton Del Ruth.
With Marie Dressler, Mabel Normand, and Mack Swain.

December

34. *Getting Acquainted* (1 reel)
    Written and directed by Charles Chaplin.
    With Mabel Normand.
35. *His Prehistoric Past* (2 reels)
    Written and directed by Charles Chaplin.
    With Mack Swain.

ESSANAY COMPANY—1915–16

(All films were written and directed by Charles Chaplin with Rollie
Totheroh as photographer.)

February

1. *His New Job* (2 reels)
   With Ben Turpin.
2. *A Night Out* (2 reels)
   With Ben Turpin.

March

3. *The Champion* (2 reels)
   With Edna Purviance.
4. *In the Park* (1 reel)
   With Edna Purviance.

April

5. *The Jitney Elopement* (2 reels)
   With Edna Purviance.
6. *The Tramp* (2 reels)
   With Edna Purviance.
7. *By the Sea* (2 reels)
   With Edna Purviance.

June

8. *Work* (2 reels)
   With Edna Purviance.

July

9. *A Woman* (2 reels)

August

10. *The Bank* (2 reels)
    With Edna Purviance.

October

11. *Shanghaied* (2 reels)
    With Edna Purviance.

November

12. *A Night in the Show* (2 reels)
    (Chaplin in dual role.)

March 1916

13. *Police* (2 reels)
    With Edna Purviance.

April 1916

14. *Carmen* (4 reels)
    With Edna Purviance and Ben Turpin.

August 1918

15. *Triple Trouble* (2 reels)
    (Salvaged by Essanay from an unfinished work by Chaplin called
    Life. Leo White added scenes in 1918.)
    With Edna Purviance.

MUTUAL COMPANY—1916–17

(All comedies were written and directed by Charles Chaplin with Rollie Totheroh as photographer. Only two-reel films were created in
this period.)

May

1. *The Floorwalker*
   With Edna Purviance and Eric Campbell.

June

2. *The Fireman*
   With Edna Purviance and Eric Campbell.

July

3. *The Vagabond*
   With Edna Purviance and Eric Campbell.

August

4. *One A.M.*
   (A solo performance by Chaplin.)

September

5. *The Count*
   With Edna Purviance and Eric Campbell.

October

6. *The Pawnshop*
   With Edna Purviance, Henry Bergman,
   and Eric Campbell.

November

7. *Behind the Screen*
   With Eric Campbell and Edna Purviance.

December

8. *The Rink*
   With Edna Purviance and Eric Campbell.

January 1917

9. *Easy Street*
   With Eric Campbell and Edna Purviance.

April

10. *The Cure*
    With Eric Campbell and Edna Purviance.

June

11. *The Immigrant*
    With Edna Purviance and Eric Campbell.

October

12. *The Adventurer*
    With Edna Purviance, Eric Campbell,
    and Henry Bergman.

FIRST NATIONAL FILM COMPANY—1918–22

(Written and directed by Charles Chaplin. Cameraman, Rollie Totheroh)

April 1918

1. *A Dog's Life* (3 reels)
   Assistant director, Chuck Riesner.
   With Edna Purviance, Sidney Chaplin, and Henry Bergman.

Fall 1918

2. *The Bond* (Half-reel)
   (A patriotic film for Liberty Loan Committee.)
   With Edna Purviance.

October 1918

3. *Shoulder Arms* (3 reels)
   With Sidney Chaplin and Edna Purviance.

June 1919

4. *Sunnyside* (3 reels)
   With Edna Purviance.

December 1919

5. *A Day's Pleasure*
   With Edna Purviance.

February 1921

6. *The Kid* (6 reels)
   Associate director Chuck Riesner.
   With Jackie Coogan and Edna Purviance.

September 1921

7. *The Idle Class* (2 reels)
   With Edna Purviance and Mack Swain.

April 1922

8. *Pay Day* (2 reels)
   With Phyllis Allen, Mack Swain, and Edna Purviance.

February 1923

9. *The Pilgrim* (4 reels)
   Associate director Chuck Riesner.
   With Edna Purviance and Mack Swain.

UNITED ARTISTS COMPANY—1923–52

(Chaplin wrote and directed all the films of this period; all were features.)

October 1923

1. *A Woman of Paris* (8 reels)

(A serious film, Chaplin played only a bit part—the station porter.)
Assistant director, Eddie Sutherland.
With Edna Purviance and Adolphe Menjou.

August 1925

2. *The Gold Rush* (9 reels)
Associate directors Charles Riesner and H. d'Abbadie d'Arrast.
Photographed by Rollie Totheroh and Jack Wilson.
With Mack Swain, Tom Murray, Georgia Hale and Henry Bergman.

(In 1926 Chaplin attempted to produce *The Sea Gull* starring Edna Purviance with Josef von Sternberg as director. Dissatisfied with the results of the scenes shot, he shelved the picture. In the twenties he also contemplated the enactment of the role of Napoleon in a serious film, but never developed the idea.)

January 1928

3. *The Circus* (7 reels)
Assistant director Harry Crocker.
Photography by Rollie Totheroh.
Cameramen Jack Wilson and Mark Marklatt.
With Merna Kennedy, Allan Garcia, and Henry Bergman.

February 1931

4. *City Lights* (9 reels)
Assistant directors Harry Crocker, Henry Bergman, and Albert Austin
Photography by Rollie Totheroh, Gordon Pollock, and Mark Marklatt.
Music composed by Charles Chaplin.
With Virginia Cherrill, Harry Meyers, and Hank Mann.

February 1936

5. *Modern Times* (9 reels)
Assistant directors Carter De Haven and Henry Bergman.
Photography by Rollie Totheroh and Ira Morgan.
Music composed by Charles Chaplin.
With Paulette Goddard, Chester Conklin, Henry Bergman, and Allan Garcia.

October 1940

6. *The Great Dictator* (126 minutes)
Assistant directors Dan James, Wheeler Dryden, and Bob Meltzer.
Photography by Karl Struss and Rollie Totheroh.

With Paulette Goddard, Jack Oakie, Reginald Gardiner, Henry Daniell, and Billy Gilbert.

(In the early forties Chaplin wanted to film Paul Vincent Carroll's stage play, *Shadow and Substance,* with Oona O'Neill portraying the leading role of Brigid. The project never materialized; he married Miss O'Neill on June 16, 1943.)

April 1947

7. *Monsieur Verdoux* (122 minutes)
   Associate directors Robert Florey and Wheeler Dryden.
   Photography by Curt Courant, Roland Totheroh, and Wallace Chewing.
   Music composed by Charles Chaplin.
   With Martha Raye, Isobel Elsom, Marilyn Nash, and Robert Lewis.

October 1952

8. *Limelight* (143 minutes)
   Assistant director Robert Aldrich.
   Photography by Karl Struss.
   Music by Charles Chaplin.
   With Claire Bloom, Sydney Chaplin, Nigel Bruce, and Buster Keaton.

ARCHWAY FILMS

September 1957

A King in New York (105 minutes)
Written, produced, and directed by Charles Chaplin.
Photography by Georges Perinal.
Music by Charles Chaplin.
With Dawn Addams, Michael Chaplin, and Maxine Audley.

UNIVERSAL

March 1967

A Countess from Hong Kong (120 minutes)
Written and directed by Charles Chaplin.
Assistant director Jack Causey.
Photography by Arthur Ibbetson.
Music by Charles Chaplin.
With Marlon Brando, Sophia Loren, and Margaret Rutherford.

Selected Bibliography

The following list presents writings that are complementary to those reprinted in this study of Chaplin. They include mainly evaluations, although some touch on the personal life of the comedian. The reader should also refer to the footnotes that appear at the beginning of the sections in this volume. Because of their special value, a few books have been included in this listing even though excerpts from them have been reprinted in the main body of this study.

BOOKS

Brownlow, Kevin. *The Parade's Gone By.* . . . New York: Knopf, 1968.
  Nostalgic, vivid interviews and evaluations of silent screen actors, directors, and technicians.

Chaplin, Charles. *Charlie Chaplin's Own Story.* Indianapolis: Bobbs-Merrill, 1916.
  A blend of fact and fiction, this personal account of the comedian's early life, stage, and screen experiences is a rare collector's item.

———. *My Autobiography.* London: Bodley Head, 1964.
  Although flooded with "famous people I have known" accounts, there are some personal reflections on his own life and works that make the book worth reading.

———. *My Trip Abroad.* New York: Harper, 1922.
  An effusive view by the comedian of meeting the public and distinguished admirers during his European tour.

Cotes, Peter, and Thelma Niklaus. *The Little Fellow.* New York: Citadel, 1965.
  Both his life and works analyzed; updated from the original 1951 publication by Philosophical Library, Inc.

Durgnat, Raymond. *The Crazy Mirror; Hollywood Comedy and the American Image.* London: Faber and Faber, 1969.
  By using sociological and comic theory concepts, an attempt to analyze the total history of comedy in the U.S.

Eastman, Max. *Great Companions.* New York: Farrar, Straus, and Cudahy, 1959.
Contains a chapter that reflects on the personality of Chaplin and defends his political views.

Fowler, Gene. *Father Goose; The Story of Mack Sennett.* New York: Corici Friede, 1934.
Focusing on the famous director's career, the book presents views on his relationship with Chaplin (pp. 228–46 and 285–87) that make interesting reading even though errors creep into the author's account.

Delluc, Louis. *Charlie Chaplin.* Translated by Hamish Miles. London: Bodley Head, 1922.
One of the first, major studies of the comedian's life and works.

Franklin, Joe. *Classics of the Silent Screen.* New York: Citadel, 1959.
Attempting to evaluate fifty films and seventy-five stars, the analyses of *The Gold Rush, City Lights,* and Chaplin become very sketchy.

Huff, Theodore. *Charlie Chaplin.* New York: Henry Schuman, 1951.
By far one of the most thorough studies of the comedian's work with a factual background on his stormy life.

Lahue, Kalton C. *World of Laughter; The Motion Picture Comedy Short, 1910–1930.* Norman, Okla.: University of Oklahoma Press, 1966.
This investigation of the total milieu of the short analyzes some of Chaplin's films, pp. 146–50.

McDonald, Gerald D., et al. *The Films of Charlie Chaplin.* New York: Citadel, 1965.
With many rare stills, this book provides summaries of plots and reviews.

Minney, Rubeigh James. *Chaplin, The Immortal Tramp.* London: G. Newnes, 1954.
Another overall study with effective synthesis of previously expressed views on Chaplin in some portions of the study.

Montgomery, John. *Comedy Films.* London: George Allen and Unwin, 1954.
One of the earliest and best evaluations of the genre's history.

Payne, Robert. *The Great God Pan; A Biography of the Tramp Played by Charles Chaplin.* New York: Hermitage House, 1952.
Even though this critic sometimes presents vague, rhapsodic interpretations, he often provides keen insights into the portrait of the Little Fellow.

Platt, Frank C. *Great Stars of Hollywood's Golden Age.* New York: The New American Library, 1966.

Drawing from his public relations position with the comedian, Carlyle R. Robinson presents some fascinating reading in an article called "The Private Life of Charlie Chaplin," pp. 71–119.

Robinson, David. *The Great Funnies; a History of Film Comedy.* London: Studio Vista, 1969.
A sketchy attempt to trace the development of the genre, but some views on the formative period are informative.

Sennett, Mack, and Cameron Shipp. *King of Comedy.* Garden City, N.Y.: Doubleday, 1954.
As inaccurate and disorganized as this reflective biography is, some good material on the director's working method and his relationship with Chaplin make it an interesting work.

Tyler, Parker. *Magic and Myth of the Movies.* Henry Holt, 1947.
The chapter, "High, Low, Comedy Jack, and the Game," contains a search for archetypes in the portraits by many comedians and in the film, *City Lights.*

Quigly, Isabel. *Charlie Chaplin; Early Comedies.* London: Studio Vista, 1968.
Too thin in detail and analysis of short films, but a good view on the development of "the legend" of Charlie.

ARTICLES

Agee, James. "Comedy's Greatest Era," *Life,* September 5, 1949, pp. 70–88.
A famous critic's skilled analyses of major silent screen comedians.

Atkinson, Brooks. "Beloved Vagabond," *The New York Times,* February 16, 1936, sec. 9, p. 1, col. 1–3.
A stage critic's affectionate reflection on the actor's early works with a brief view on *Modern Times.*

Beaumont, Charles. "Chaplin" *Playboy,* March 1960, pp. 81–89.
A sympathetic view on the comedian's personal problems with women, the press, the public, and the government.

Capp, A. "The Comedy of Charlie Chaplin," *Atlantic Monthly,* February 1950, pp. 25–29.
A limited, oversimplified application of comic theory by the famous cartoonist.

Cooke, Alistair. "Charlie Chaplin," *Atlantic Monthly,* August 1939, pp. 176–85.
An overall evaluation with some good information on production methods of *The Great Dictator.*

"Comedy Has its Limits," *Christian Century,* June 26, 1940, pp. 816–17.
An unsigned, negative editorial stating that Hitler was too great a menace to be the subject of the comedy, *The Great Dictator.*

Hickey, Terry. "Accusations against Charles Chaplin for Political and Moral Offenses," *Film Comment,* Winter 1969, pp. 44–56.
A vital, well-researched article on the actor's personal problems.

Meryman, Richard. "Interview of Chaplin," *Life,* March 10, 1967, pp. 82–84, 88–94.
One of the best interviews to reveal that the actor-director held to some of his basic theories and working methods of the past.

Rosen, Philip. "The Chaplin World-View," *Cinema Journal,* Fall 1969, pp. 2–12.
An effective, scholarly attempt to investigate the thinking of the artist.

Seldes, Gilbert. "A Chaplin Masterpiece," *New Republic,* February 25, 1931, pp. 46–47.
A rave review of *City Lights.*

Spears, Jack. "Chaplin Collaborators," *Films in Review,* January 1962, pp. 18–36.
With a carping attitude, the writer examines those who assisted in the creative process.

Van Doren, Mark. "Charlie Chaplin," *Nation,* February 18, 1936, p. 232.
A favorable review declaring that *Modern Times* is a work of laughter and not social comment.

Wallach, George. "Charlie Chaplin's *Monsieur Verdoux* Press Conference," *Film Comment,* Winter 1969, pp. 34–42.
A fascinating transcription to the page of a preserved taped press conference which developed into an attack on the actor.

Wilson, Edmund. "The New Chaplin Comedy," *New Republic,* September 2, 1925, pp. 45–46.
The famous literary critic's view of *The Gold Rush* with a focus on the skilled use of gags.

Young, Stark. "Dear Mr. Chaplin," *New Republic,* August 23, 1922, pp. 358–59.
A curious article with the proposition that the comedian should abandon his trivial stories and act in films adapted from worthy legitimate stage dramas.

———. "Charlie Chaplin," *New Republic,* February 8, 1928, pp. 313–14.
This review notes the artist's return to his earlier type of comedy blended with "pathos."

Index

FILM FOCUS

Ronald Gottesman and Harry M. Geduld
General Editors

COM